GIVE ME YOUR HAND

Traditional and Practical Guidance on Visiting the Sick
Second Edition

BIKKUR CHOLIM
בִּקּוּר חוֹלִים

Jane Handler

Kim Hetherington

with Rabbi Stuart L. Kelman

Originally published by Adas Israel Congregation,
Washington, D.C., 1988

Second edition published by Congregation Netivot Shalom,
Berkeley, California, 1997

FOR INFORMATION CONTACT:

THE NATIONAL CENTER FOR JEWISH HEALING
(JBFC) 120 W. 57th Street
New York, NY 10019

CONGREGATION NETIVOT SHALOM
1841 Berkeley Way
Berkeley, CA 94703

TO ORDER ADDITIONAL COPIES:

EKS PUBLISHING
322 Castro Street
Oakland, CA 94607
(510) 251-9100 · Fax (510) 251-9102

PREFACE

My friend Tina Lorris died of cancer in March 1986. She was 48. Tina lived to the hilt even while she was dying. She helped me to understand that in sharing myself with a seriously ill friend, I was helping to enhance the increasingly limited quality of her life.

After Tina's death, Rabbi Avis Miller of Adas Israel Congregation in Washington, D.C., also a close friend of Tina, wished to honor Tina's memory in a special way. She asked me to coordinate a symposium on *bikkur cholim*, the *mitzvah* of visiting the sick, in which the congregation could participate and which would address congregants' concerns about performing this difficult and often stressful *mitzvah*.

The response to the symposium was so positive that Rabbi Miller asked Kim Hetherington and me to develop the material from the transcript into a booklet, *Give Me Your Hand*. Writing the booklet with Kim was a privilege. The preparation for the Nathan Cummings Foundation of a revised edition that includes the enriching contributions of Rabbi Stuart Kelman is especially rewarding and provides a spiritual and practical tribute to Tina Lorris' memory that, I believe, she would have appreciated.

Jane Handler
Washington, D.C.
Shavuot 5757

THANK YOU

In Metropolitan Washington, D.C.: Kerry Roberts Manson, Ph.D.; Shirley Papilsky, M.D., Paul Rhodes, M.D.; Gail Schwartz, Chair, Adas Israel *Bikkur Cholim* Committee; Robert Siegel, M.D.; C. L. Vordenbaum, M.S.W., M.C.S.W. (author of the section on AIDS); and Elizabeth Weiss, R.N.

At the Nathan Cummings Foundation: Rabbi Rachel Cowan.

At Congregation Netivot Shalom: Denah S. Bookstein, Alison Jordan, Elana Kelman, Barbara Peleg, Jane Rubin, Miriam Shein, and Danielle Shelley.

At the National Center for Jewish Healing: Rabbi Simkha Weintraub and David Hirsh.

3

FOREWORD

"IT IS A *MITZVAH* TO VISIT THE SICK" (SHULCHAN ARUCH YOREH DEAH 335:1). PLAIN, simple and direct. Whether mandated by Judaism or dictated by the mores of society, the *mitzvah* of *bikkur cholim*, visiting the sick, is directed at all of us regardless of position, status, or gender. It is both participatory and egalitarian.

Illness, whether our own or that of someone we care for, has a way of focusing our attention on essential issues by calling into question the conventional beliefs we use to hide our vulnerability. Illness punctures our defenses, leaves us wide open and exposed to a welter of emotions; we are prey to our imagination and to our fears, we feel weak and powerless.[1]

Rabbi Harold Kushner suggests that the person who asks, "Why is this happening to me?" can be compared to a friend who says to you, "What did I ever do to deserve this?" This person doesn't really want a list of things he or she did to deserve this. In much the same way, neither does the person asking why want an explanation. What is being requested is simple reassurance that he or she is a good person and doesn't deserve it.

Healing does not always mean curing the body. Healing may take the form of resolving family rifts, giving or receiving forgiveness, allowing the patient to die with peace of mind, or the eventual reconciliation of family and friends who suffer the pain of loss.

Rabbi Harold Schulweis once suggested that the underlying ethos of *bikkur cholim* is the dignity of the human being, the respect for his or her suffering, and the power of community to restore dignity to the patient.

It is with this in mind that Congregation Netivot Shalom in Berkeley, California, began the creation of its **Chevrat Bikkur Cholim**, its *Bikkur Cholim* Society. At its inception we came upon the wonderful manual, *Give Me Your Hand*, which originated at Adas Israel Congregation in Washington, D.C. We asked for permission to adapt it for our purposes. We then approached the Nathan Cummings Foundation, which made

4

it possible for this pamphlet to be published. Distribution was provided for by the Central Conference of American Rabbis, the Rabbinical Assembly, the Reconstructionist Rabbinical Association, the Jewish Theological Seminary of America, the Hebrew Union College-Jewish Institute of Religion, the Reconstructionist Rabbinical College, and the University of Judaism. This is a remarkable *shidduch*, and our thanks go to these institutions.

May we all be privileged to participate in this act of *chesed*, uniting our actions with those of God.

Rabbi Stuart L. Kelman
Congregation Netivot Shalom
Berkeley, California
Shavuot 5757

TABLE OF CONTENTS

CHAPTER I

BIKKUR CHOLIM—
A FUNDAMENTAL
OBLIGATION OF JEWISH LAW

LTHOUGH MOST OF US DO NOT HESITATE TO VISIT CLOSE FRIENDS AND FAMILY members when they become ill, we are not always comfortable doing it. We are even less comfortable at the prospect of visiting casual friends or strangers. Often we convince ourselves that visiting those who are ill would be an intrusion on their privacy. We resist confronting the patient's pain and vulnerability because we feel unable to make things better. But when we ask whether to proceed with visiting despite any qualms, Jewish tradition answers us with an emphatic yes.

Give Me Your Hand provides the reader with both traditional and modern guidance for visiting family, friends, or strangers who are ill. It explains the theological and historical roots of *bikkur cholim,* the *mitzvah* of visiting the sick, traces the performance of the *mitzvah* in traditional observance and modern practice, and answers the most common questions about tending to the needs of persons with serious injuries and illnesses.

Why consider the historical and theological aspects of the *mitzvah?* Because by integrating the historical perspective into any performance of *bikkur cholim,* our actions assume a continuity across time and space, between the mundane and the divinely inspired. We become more confident visitors and better Jews.

9

THE TORAH—ULTIMATE SOURCE OF MORAL GUIDANCE

The Torah, the first five books of the Bible, is the ultimate source of the law on which Jews rely for moral guidance. Rabbis and teachers through the ages have interpreted and codified this law so that generations of Jews might better understand and live by it.

The Torah commands Jews to "walk after Adonai Your God,"[2] that is, to emulate God's attributes. Significantly, the Hebrew for "walk" comes from the same root as *halachah*, "law." Jews become holy, literally, by "walking" God's law.

After creating the beasts of the earth, God said, "Let us make 'Adam' [humankind] in our image, after our likeness."[3] According to the rabbis, to be made "in God's image" is to do things as God has done them, to follow God's example.

God visited the sick: "And Adonai appeared to him in the oaks of Mamre."[4] According to rabbinic interpretation, God visited Abraham at Mamre as Abraham was recovering from his circumcision. From this extraordinary occurrence, the rabbis derived the importance of *bikkur cholim*—visiting the sick. "Just as God visited the sick, so too, you should visit the sick."[5]

Visiting the sick is one of a number of acts which permits us to achieve holiness because, according to the Torah, God either did them personally or commanded the Jews, as the chosen people, to do them. The effect of extending ourselves to others through certain actions is to perpetuate a sense of community. Community itself is a concept integral to traditional Jewish life.

TRADITIONAL SOURCES OF GUIDANCE FOR FULFILLING THE MITZVAH OF BIKKUR CHOLIM

The Torah does not provide any practical guidance for the performance of the *mitzvah*. Other sources—mainly rabbinic—give practical guidance as to what God expects of us in fulfilling it.

Two principal categories of rabbinic writings have informed Jewish practice of *mitzvot* over the centuries—*halachah* (law) and *aggadah* (lore). Jewish tradition considers *halachah* and *aggadah* to be inspired by Torah.

ACTS OF LOVING-KINDNESS—*GEMILUT CHASADIM*

The rabbis have designated visiting the sick as one of several acts of loving-kindness (*gemilut chasadim*)—basic communal obligations of Judaism. A daily prayer states:

> These are the things of which a person enjoys the fruits in this world, while the principal remains in the hereafter, namely: honoring father and mother, practice of kindness, hospitality to strangers, visiting the sick, dowering the bride, attending the dead to the grave...but study of Torah exceeds them all.[6]

This prayer gives powerful expression to the idea that doing God's work on earth (*tikkun olam*) makes that work holy. The medieval code of laws, the Shulchan Aruch, states simply and bluntly that "it is a religious duty to visit the sick."[7]

Recognizing, however, how difficult God's work can be for all of us, the rabbis have carefully described rewards in this life and the hereafter. A person who helps others enjoys the fruits of his or her deeds during a lifetime, as this is a contribution to the well-being and continuity of the community. Also, a person who visits the sick can derive satisfaction from the expectation that the community will reciprocate this act.[8]

BIKKUR CHOLIM—AN IMPERATIVE OF JEWISH TRADITION

The rabbis believe that by visiting the sick we bring them both physical and psychological healing. According to the Talmud (Nedarim 39b), Rabbi Akiva visited a disciple who became ill and whom no one else would visit. Akiva entered the man's house and "swept and sprinkled the ground before him." When the man recovered, he acknowledged that Akiva had revived him. Akiva immediately lectured his disciples, saying, "One who does not visit the sick is like a shedder of blood."[9] In other words, our visits to a sick person make such a significant difference to recovery that to refrain from this obligation is to prolong the illness.

In performing *bikkur cholim*, we foster the Jewish reverence for life. Akiva's statement underscores the contemporary relevance of ancient and medieval rabbinic teaching about the importance of *bikkur cholim*.

Another sage, Rabbi Yochanan, said to his friend Rabbi Elazar, who was seriously ill, "Give me your hand." Rabbi Elazar gave Rabbi Yochanan his hand, and Rabbi Yochanan raised him.[10] The rabbis teach that a sick person cannot heal himself but needs the help of others. Therefore, one who performs *bikkur cholim* helps to heal a sick person.

Those who visit a sick person are considered blessed because they remove "a sixtieth part of the sickness."[11] The importance of each individual in healing an afflicted person cannot be overestimated. The rabbis emphasize, however, that while each visitor removes a sixtieth part of the remaining illness, the illness could never reach zero unless the sick person participates in his or her own healing.

Jewish tradition teaches that it is important to allow others to help us when we are sick. According to *midrash*, Rabbi Yochanan visited Rabbi Chanina during the latter's illness. When Rabbi Chanina complained about his suffering, Rabbi Yochanan suggested that he speak the same encouraging words to himself that he had spoken with such good effect to Rabbi Yochanan when he was ill. Rabbi Chanina replied, "When I was free of sufferings, I could help others; but now that I am myself a sufferer, I must ask others to help me."[12] The meaning of this story is obvious but bears repeating: we should know both how to give and how to take, and that in taking, often we are also giving.

THE LIMITS OF *BIKKUR CHOLIM*

There are situations, however, where despite the seriousness of the illness and urgency of the need, tradition prohibits visiting.

Visiting enemies. There is controversy among scholars about whether one should visit an enemy who falls sick. One argument against visiting an enemy who is ill or in mourning is that a person could create an impression of gloating over another's misfortune, thereby causing depression in the person being visited. In other words, if it is impossible to convey empathy and concern to a sick person, it is best to stay away.[13]

Persons with contagious diseases. Because of the *halachic* prohibition of behavior that endangers one's own life,[14] we are not encouraged to visit where direct contact could cause the visitor to become seriously ill. This is not to be construed as an excuse to avoid visiting, but rather as a prevention against endangering one's own life.

Where conversation is injurious. Tradition forbids visiting a person with a severe headache, because visiting might cause an intense strain.[15] This restriction applies by analogy to any visit during which conversation, of itself, would be injurious to health.

Persons with embarrassing afflictions. The Shulchan Aruch forbids visits to persons with eye and bowel diseases. Apparently these were considered diseases which cause embarrassment to the afflicted person.[16] While eye disease may not cause embarrassment, as with a headache, speaking may be difficult. Today, the list of embarrassing conditions varies among cultures, age groups, and even economic classes. The tradition, however, reflects a general sensitivity to the fact that if the patient would be embarrassed on account of the illness, it is advisable not to visit.

CHAPTER II

THE PERFORMANCE OF BIKKUR CHOLIM

OW DO YOU DECIDE WHETHER TO VISIT SOMEONE WHO IS SICK? MANY traditional sources address this question. Although there is no causal relationship between ancient and modern practices of visiting the sick, rabbinic responses generally correlate well with modern medical practice.

Certainly the purpose of *bikkur cholim* as expressed by the rabbis of earlier eras is unchanged: not simply to comfort the sick, but actually to promote healing, by reinforcing connections to life and to a caring community, and to pray.

At best, the caring community of a patient consists of family and friends, as well as those who visit the sick for the sake of the *mitzvah*. In fact, since geography often separates us from family and friends, and because people sometimes outlive their loved ones, the visitor may be the sole representative of the caring community.

HOW TO PERFORM *BIKKUR CHOLIM*

It has always been important to let a sick person know that the community remembers and cares. This message is often conveyed through shared emotions and mutuality—for example, by laughing or crying together. The Talmud tells of Rabbi Yochanan's empathetic visit to his student, Rabbi Elazar, who was ill. Rabbi Yochanan noticed that he was crying. Rabbi Elazar told Rabbi Yochanan that he mourned because Rabbi Yochanan, an incredibly handsome as well as a warm and caring man, would some day die. Rabbi Yochanan responded, "Well dost thou weep on that account," and the two friends cried together.[17]

THE INITIAL VISIT

The tradition. According to tradition, relatives and friends may visit the patient as soon as illness strikes; strangers may visit after three days. If the sickness is sudden and appears to be serious, all may visit immediately. The rule recognizes that unless there are exceptional circumstances, those closest to a person who falls ill are most likely to be needed during the early stages of illness. The rest of the community is not, however, absolved from its obligations merely because a person has relatives and friends.[18]

Modern practice. Generally, only immediate family members and intimate friends are appropriate visitors in a sickroom during the first twenty-four hours of a medical crisis, although if the situation is deemed terminal, a wider circle of friends and relatives might be admitted. When a person is critically ill, the decision regarding who can visit must be made by the patient's physician and the closest member of the patient's circle. There is a chance—albeit small—that upon seeing so many familiar faces, the patient will suspect the worst and despair.

Unless you have a close relationship, you should wait several days before visiting people who have suffered disorienting or disfiguring medical crises or procedures, such as drug overdoses; radical chemotherapy; automobile accidents; surgery to the face, neck, or head; or strokes.

If a family member or friend has assumed the role of "gatekeeper" for the patient, it is politic to ask when you might visit. If that person rebuffs you, inquire of the hospital staff whether there is a medical reason for the refusal to grant you access to the patient. If there is not, perhaps you could ask the staff to point out that your visit would be harmless at the least, and therapeutic at best. If you are still denied access, you must accept the situation.

More often there is no "gatekeeper" and the patient is able to make a decision on whom to admit and when. Call or write a note to introduce yourself if the patient is not a close friend, wish him or her well, and inquire when you might visit. Agree on a mutually convenient time.

Remember that hospital patients must surrender a great deal of the control they normally exercise over their lives to hospital staff. They often must depend on nurses and doctors for various treatments and comfort. Hospital routine encourages passivity. Frequently, a patient's personality and behavior change in response to this environment, and this change may surprise and disconcert you on your first visit.

If the patient refuses to see you initially, do not take this as a personal rejection. Very likely the refusal reflects a sensitivity about his or her condition or appearance. Wish the patient well, and leave your number with the nursing staff in case the patient changes his or her mind about a visit. Do not abandon the patient at this point! A few days later, call or send a card with a note. Repeat your interest in visiting and enclose your telephone number.

If the patient refuses to have you visit, respect these wishes, but send an occasional card as a reminder that the hand of friendship is still open. Refusal, however, is the exception. Most patients, bored by the hospital or home routine, welcome visitors. Their humanity is reinforced by your visit.

If possible, familiarize yourself with the patient's medical situation so that you will not appear surprised or shocked if the patient is disfigured or disabled. Remember that regardless of the medical condition, the patient wants to be treated like the person he or she has always been and expects to be upon recovery. Avoid pity or condescension. The person is more than the illness.

Enter the room with something to talk about—news of the community or the world, or a topic of particular interest to the patient or to you. Do not bring up your own medical problems or the illnesses of others.

Take a small gift—a newspaper, magazine, candy bar, or game—to ease your initial encounter. Do not wear perfume or shaving lotion, because illness often heightens a person's sense of smell, and strong odors may be unpleasant. Always wash your hands before and after visiting.

Do not be afraid of doing something wrong. After all, the situation is new to both of you. Mistakes are inevitable; be forthright about them. Mistakes can be helpful if they bond people together.

Do not make elaborate plans for your initial visit. Sometimes, extensive anticipation and planning can result in your actually doing nothing. Inaction is contrary to Jewish tradition. "It is not incumbent on you to complete the work, but neither are you free to desist from it."[19]

Finally, prepare yourself for the visit psychologically and spiritually. You may want to take a moment to center yourself before ringing the bell or entering the room. If you feel comfortable doing so, you may want to recite a spontaneous prayer or a psalm to accomplish this purpose. Pray for yourself, others you love, medical personnel, spiritual teachers—as appropriate and helpful to you. There are audio tapes available to assist you as well.

THE APPROPRIATE TIME TO VISIT

The tradition. Regarding the appropriate time of day to visit, the Shulchan Aruch specifies that "One must not visit the sick during the first three hours of the day—for every invalid's illness is alleviated in the morning, and [consequently] one will not be troubled to pray for him or her; and not during the last three hours of the day—for then the illness grows worse and one will give up hope to pray."[20]

Visiting the sick on the Sabbath is considered an excellent and appropriate use of this holy day.

Modern practice. For therapeutic reasons, hospital visiting hours are generally during the middle of the day and in the early evening. In the early morning, the patient is likely to be sore and disheveled and might be confronting the prospect of physically or emotionally distressing treatment. In the evening, pain tends to be worse. Therefore, the visitor is well advised to respect standard visiting hours, even after the patient is back home. Mealtime is often an excellent opportunity to visit someone in the hospital. Patients do not always enjoy eating alone. Your presence may distract from the usual mundane quality of the food and may actually encourage eating.

Furthermore, when a patient undergoes certain treatments, such as chemotherapy, it is important to inquire of the staff if visitors can come at all on a treatment day.

LENGTH AND FREQUENCY OF VISITS

The tradition. Tradition encourages frequent visits. Raba says, "One must visit even a hundred times a day, so long as the visitor does not trouble the sick person."[21] The rabbis recognize both the patient's desire for the attention of visitors and his or her right to privacy.

Modern practice. Kindness and common sense require that you visit a sick person not only while in the hospital but during the longer time of convalescence at home. Indeed, the convalescent period might be when there is the greatest need for the *mitzvah*. While someone is in the hospital, however unpleasant the experience might be, he or she is surrounded by other people and the bustle of hospital routine; it is later, when the crisis is past but recovery incomplete, that a person is often forgotten and left alone.

Whether in the hospital or at home, your visits should be brief. Indeed, it is better to visit several times or even frequently for brief periods than to spend one long period of time with a patient. When in doubt about how long to stay, leave early. Often the patient will say, "It's nice that you've taken the time to come visit." This may be a clue to leave.

Of course, there are times when a longer visit is appropriate, such as when you travel a long distance and can stay in the area only a limited time. Also, there are instances when patients request frequent or even constant companionship.

Keep in mind that the hospital patient may not simply be waiting for visits, however welcome they might be. On the contrary, there are many tasks and demands on the patient: coping with pain and treatment, dealing with the hospital environment and staff, preserving an emotional balance and satisfactory self-image, and preserving a relationship with family and close friends. Only after contending with all of this can the patient attend to the casual visitor, even if the visit is the least demanding, most enlivening aspect of the day.

If, upon arrival, you discover that the patient has one or more visitors, ask whether you might come back at another time. If a doctor comes in to examine the patient during your visit, leave spontaneously. If the visit has already gone on for awhile, say good-bye, "until next time." If your visit has just begun, offer to wait outside in the hall and return when the examination is over. Upon your return, be sensitive: did the patient undergo an uncomfortable procedure? If you suspect that this is the case, find out if the patient would prefer that you visit at another time.

When you leave, do not ask, "Would you like me to come again?" for the patient might not want to infringe on your time. In this debilitated condition, he or she might feel unworthy of your efforts. Say, rather, "I'd like to visit again if you'd like me to come."

If you visit in a hospital and find the patient asleep, leave a note either at the bedside or at the nurses' station. You also might want to include a prayer for a *refuah shelaymah* רְפוּאָה שְׁלֵמָה—a complete healing, along with a *Mi Sheberach*, a copy of which can be found in the back in Appendix 1.

Remember that periodic or even frequent visits benefit the patient both indirectly and directly. They establish the patient's identity in the eyes of the hospital staff, who are reminded that the patient is a beloved member of a family and the community. Such reminders to the staff are particularly important where the patient is unable to express his or her own identity because of coma, dementia, paralysis, other severe disabilities, or because he or she is of a shy disposition.

LISTENING

The tradition. Tradition teaches us that even when someone is too sick to visit face-to-face, we should stand outside the door to hear the sounds of suffering.[22] Understanding what the patient is experiencing is critical. If the person visited desires to talk about the illness or any other concerns, the visitor should listen carefully. If, however, the patient is too ill to speak, the visitor should sit quietly with the person and try to imagine his or her suffering. This is an opportunity truly to "be present" with the patient.

Modern practice. Your most important task in visiting the sick is to listen to the patient. Listening should be active; that is, you should confirm, acknowledge, reflect, and perhaps even question what the patient is telling you. Frequently, a seriously ill patient's first theme is anger towards God or the physicians. If the patient cannot rail against God, dare not criticize the physician, and does not want to burden the family with feelings of anger, he or she may direct the anger towards a stranger or casual friend.

Let this anger come out. Don't take it personally or withdraw. If the patient complains about God or fate, sympathize, but do not engage in theological speculation or advice. Although you are doing God's work, you are not a spiritual counselor. Although you are in partnership with God, God can defend God's self.

If the patient is angry over medical decisions, express sympathy but remain impartial. Most persons, unfamiliar with the specifics of a person's condition, cannot evaluate the pros and cons of a medical decision. Particularly if you are a trained physician, your expression of doubt or disagreement with the decision of the primary physician may confirm the patient's fears and inhibit recovery.

Likewise, acknowledge the person's pain but remain impartial if, under the stress of the illness, the patient expresses anger towards family and close friends. Ultimately the patient will appreciate your listening but not taking sides. It is often difficult to maintain neutrality in the face of someone's anger or complaints and, within the boundaries of confidentiality, you may want to "debrief" with the rabbi or *Bikkur Cholim* Committee.

Listening carefully to the patient eases your task as a visitor by providing clues as to what to talk about subsequently and what things will distract the patient from his or her condition. Remember that you are there as a friend. Do not feel that you have to make things better. Unless specifically asked to share a piece of information, consider everything you hear to be confidential.

TALKING

The tradition. Because Judaism is life-oriented, the visitor's mission is not to console the patient or to counsel him or her to accept this illness. The visitor is expected to reach out to the sick person, to be there and express concern and offer words of encouragement that urge striving for recovery. According to a *midrash*, when Rabbi Yochanan suffered from fever, Rabbi Chanina, his teacher, visited him. When Rabbi Yochanan complained that he could not bear his illness, Rabbi Chanina urged him to say instead that God is trustworthy. When the suffering became truly unbearable, Rabbi Chanina visited again and said things to Rabbi Yochanan which are unrecorded, but which caused him to take courage.[23] Even when Rabbi Yochanan's situation was desperate, Rabbi Chanina was able to give, and Rabbi Yochanan to accept, encouraging advice.

In general, Jewish tradition views negatively any speculation about whether God might have reasons for bringing suffering upon a particular individual. The reason for this view is that such speculation is inappropriate and not directed toward healing. For example, regardless of a person's views, the visitor should never suggest to a patient that suffering is ennobling, or a deserved payment for past deeds.

In the book of Job, Job's friends tell him that he should examine his past to determine of what sins he is guilty, because God is allowing him to suffer so much. We know, however, that Job was a good man and that his suffering was not penance for past misdeeds.

So too, the *midrash* explores and often discards the notion that God chastises those God loves (*yissurim shel ahavah*) for the sake of making them stronger. When Rabbi Yochanan visited his teacher, Rabbi Chanina, during an illness, he asked, "How fares it with you?" To this Rabbi Chanina responded, "How hard are sufferings." Rabbi Yochanan mused, "How great is the reward." Rabbi Chanina answered unequivocally, "I desire neither them nor their reward."[24]

While Judaism does have a goodly number of philosophical views concerning illness, the visit is not the appropriate occasion to discuss them. The visitor who avoids philosophical or theological discussions about the cause or purpose of another's illness follows the injunction, "Give me your hand"—and thus offers unobtrusive assistance to one who is ill.

Modern practice. It is not necessary for you to talk with the patient all the time you are visiting. Sometimes your presence in the sickroom is enough. A patient who has had difficulty sleeping in the unfamiliar hospital environment might be able to drift off knowing you are sitting nearby. A patient in pain might take comfort simply from having you there. Indeed, your presence is a powerful response to the question "What to say when there is nothing to say?" That is why *bikkur cholim* is called both a "talking cure" and a "silent cure."

Watch and listen for clues from the patient regarding the desire for conversation. Let the topic emerge. When you speak, employ a friendly, gentle tone. Let your voice impart serenity. Rabbi Harold Kushner tells the story of the little boy whose mother sent him on an errand. He was a long time coming back. When he finally returned, his mother said, "Where were you? I was worried about you!" The boy replied, "Oh, there's this kid down the street whose tricycle broke and he was crying because he couldn't fix it. And I felt bad so I stopped to help him." The mother said, "Are you trying to tell me that you know how to fix a tricycle?" The boy said, "No, of course not. I simply sat down and I helped him cry."

Do not initiate discussion of the patient's medical condition. Even if you have information firsthand from the patient's physician, it is not your business to impart it. If, however, the patient wants to tell you about his or her experience, about illness or even death, be open and prepared to follow his or her lead.

In general, your conversation can expand the patient's boundaries to the world beyond the sickroom. Talk about the larger world: home and garden, neighborhood, synagogue, clubs and community, hobbies, sports, and politics. Talk about the world of the past: hometown, parents, schooling, military service, adventures, career. Also strive to give the patient a vision of the future—a vision of restored health and participation in life. Encourage thinking ahead and making plans—even for the next day or week if appropriate, unless this seems overwhelming or runs against the common need for taking "one day at a time." Try not to deny the past, but focus more on the future. If the future is indeed bleak, you may need to acknowledge that fact while at the same time helping the patient cope with the elements over which he or she does have control.

Reinforce your conversation about the world beyond the patient's room with small gifts: newspapers, magazines, cassettes of favorite music, or catalogs of courses to take (if possible) at the local Jewish or adult education program or community college.

Some say that laughter is the best medicine, so do not be afraid to laugh in the sickroom. Laughter does not deny the seriousness of a situation, and it can help the patient overcome any discomfort over altered appearances or ability to function. Laughter can also remind a patient that there is something beyond the present, unhappy moment. Here is an opportunity to reinforce the broader goal of bringing a sense of normalcy into the visit.

Remember that hearing is the last sense to go. It does no harm, and might do some good, to talk to an unresponsive patient who appears unable to hear. In the same vein, do not talk about an apparently unconscious person in his or her presence.

PRAYER

The tradition. Our tradition is very clear about prayer being an essential component of the obligation of *bikkur cholim*.[25] One should pray, the *Shulchan Aruch* teaches, either in the presence of the patient or elsewhere. Prayers in the presence of a sick person may be in the vernacular, so that they may be understood, or in Hebrew, which tradition explains is the language of the angels who bring human messages to God.[26] By reciting or offering prayers, we may stimulate hope and strength for the patient and help him or her release tension and worry. Prayer brings out the spiritual dimension to our visit.

The *Shulchan Aruch* stresses that prayers for a particular sick person should request healing for all Jewish persons who are ill.[27] Recitation in the synagogue of a blessing called *Mi Sheberach*, for the sick members of the community, has been and continues to be accepted practice.

What to pray for? At the very least, and even in the midst of an apparently hopeless situation, tradition implores the visitor to encourage the patient to hope. But what can the patient hope for? You can hope for less pain; for the happiness of a surviving mate and children; for the family's continuation of the values that the patient has taught them; for the amelioration of whatever is the most fearful of concerns;

for the power to endure what humans cannot understand; for the capacity to feel the love of family and friends; for courage; and lastly, for an awareness of God's love. Finally, Jewish tradition often affirms the belief in a life after death. The visitor who feels comfortable with this concept may want to make reference to this ultimate form of hope.[28]

Our tradition also directs the visitor to pray for healing even if a person is terminally ill. The language of the final confession offers powerful support for this viewpoint. "I pray that God will heal me, but if not, then please accept my final confession."[29] Particularly in silent prayer, outside of the patient's hearing, tradition considers it appropriate to pray that the suffering of a terminally ill person be alleviated and that the family be comforted. Finally, coupling the needs of the individual with that of the community, it is customary also to say upon leaving: הַמָּקוֹם יְרַחֵם אוֹתְךָ (אוֹתָךְ) בְּתוֹךְ שְׁאָר חוֹלֵי יִשְׂרָאֵל *hamakom yirachem otcha* (feminine: *otach*) *betoch shaar cholei yisrael* (May God have mercy on you along with the other sick of Israel).

Modern practice. The traditional concept of appropriate prayer offers the visitor guidance. Appendix 1 gives some traditional and some modern examples of prayers. Many prayer books (*siddurim*) offer other prayers suitable for the needs of one who is ill.[30]

You should pray in the sickroom only at the request of the patient and your prayer should be clearly audible. Offer to provide the patient with the necessary materials for the Sabbath and holy days, so long as the hospital permits this. If the patient accepts this offer, you might inquire whether you could join him or her. On the Sabbath and holy days, extraordinarily difficult times, your visit in order to pray with a patient would be a particular kindness. Often, simply singing a *niggun* (a melody without words), playing some music, or repeating a sentence (such as the *Sh'ma*) can bring comfort.

If you feel comfortable doing so, offer your own personal prayers. They can include words asking for both *refuat haguf*, healing of body, and *refuat hanefesh*, healing of soul. Formulating your prayers may help you to be more in touch with your feelings. At the very least, when leaving the patient's presence, you may want to wish him or her a *refuah shelaymah*, a "whole recovery." This short prayer asks God to bring healing and certainly conveys far more meaning than the usual, "take care."

It is unlikely that you, as a member of the community fulfilling the mitzvah of bikkur cholim, will be with the patient as the end draws near. If you are, however, be sensitive to the fact that some patients will feel the need for permission to die; aware of their responsibilities to their families, their friends, their communities, their God, they have to know that they might safely lay their burdens down, that they are not regarded as "abandoning" their obligations, that there are other who will shoulder them.

Persons on the brink of death sometimes seek forgiveness for acts they have committed in their past, or for the pain and trouble their illness has occasioned. Encourage the patient to speak freely about these needs, and to pray for assurance and forgiveness.

Prayer has been called a "life support." It "can bring about an emotional release and the regrouping of energies needed to face a crisis; it puts the entire situation in a broader perspective, enabling one to relate a personal nightmare to the human condition, shared by so many others. Prayer not only asks for healing but prepares one for the possibility that the request may not be granted. When the patient knows that prayers are being offered on his or her behalf, the very knowledge that other people care affords strength…prayer is a life-uplifting plea and a powerful statement of one's deepest values and concerns. We do not expect that prayer will act as an autonomous force guaranteeing recovery."[31]

TOUCHING THE SICK PERSON

The tradition. The rabbinic injunction, "Give me your hand," can be understood both in metaphoric and practical terms. Tradition teaches that the impact of bikkur cholim is to increase the physical well-being of the patient. Consequently, physical interaction is seen as an important or even critical component of healing.

Modern practice. The wisdom of the rabbi who ordered a friend, "Give me your hand," has been confirmed by modern therapeutics. The touch of a friendly hand, the caress, the kiss of friendship can be a strong stimulus to well-being. Sometimes, as in the case of a catatonic or demented patient, it is the most immediate way to communicate affection.

Be judicious in touching a sick individual, but do not shrink from it at the appropriate moment. Extending the palm of your hand, for example, rather than your fingers, affords a more secure grasp and tells the patient you are self-confident. Generally you will know when the patient is receptive to being touched; if you are in doubt, ask, "Would you like me to hold your hand?" "Would it feel good if I stroked your brow/brushed your hair/rubbed your shoulders?" Or as a parting gesture, you can suggest, by action if not by words, "Give me your hand."

Remember that the need for explicit or implicit permission to touch extends to the personal medical paraphernalia of the patient: prostheses, crutches, walkers, wheelchairs, and even furniture in the room.

SITTING WITH THE PATIENT

The tradition. Tradition teaches that the Divine Presence (*Shechinah*) hovers above the head of the sick bed.[32] The Shulchan Aruch instructs the visitor to sit reverently in front of the invalid, rather than sitting on the bed, since sitting might obstruct the Divine Presence and create the impression that it is the visitor, not God, who is the ultimate provider of health.[33] This is a statement about "bedside manner." The vertical visitor—unintentionally—lords over the horizontal patient. This Talmudic advice implies that by sitting on the same plane, both visitor and patient are under the protection of God and join in shared mortality.

Modern practice. Be sensitive to your location *vis-à-vis* the patient, particularly the bedridden patient. Avoid sitting on the bed unless the patient asks you to. Position yourself so that you can be seen and heard without strain. Be discreet about looking at your watch or the wall clock. Try to communicate a sense that, for the moments of the visit, there are no distractions or urgent commitments pulling you elsewhere.

TENDING TO TANGIBLE NEEDS

The tradition. The *mitzvah* of *bikkur cholim* obligates the community to take care of the worldly concerns of the patient and to provide essential peace of mind.[34]

Modern practice. Today, these concerns might be financial, family, or personal matters requiring performance of concrete tasks such as helping pay the bills, doing housework (like Rabbi Akiva who swept his disciple's floor!), carpooling children, or arranging transportation to the doctor.

Just as you listen for clues as to when a patient wants to talk and what to talk about, try to discover how you can be of tangible assistance. Canvass the family, friends, and hospital staff for suggestions.

Be realistic about your time. Offer to do specific things that are within your actual capacity to perform. Leave the patient free to accept or decline your offer.

One of your more useful functions is to expand the patient's boundaries beyond the hospital room or the home during convalescence. If possible, at the hospital, take him or her to the day room or out onto the grounds. Take a homebound patient into the yard, for a walk around the block, or for a drive in your car. Go to a movie, to a club meeting, to a class or lecture, or simply for a cup of coffee. Contact the patient's friends and relatives and urge them to visit or at least to call or write.

These kindnesses are particularly critical for those patients who confront an extended or permanent illness or disability at home. People in this situation may be forgotten or may put a great burden on their immediate families.

Your service as a visitor can extend to assisting the family of the patient. Knowing that someone is helping the family often proves therapeutic to the patient, alleviating some of the worry and guilt over being disabled. For example, if the patient is in intensive care for a protracted period, you might sit with family members, who often spend hours in the waiting room anticipating brief opportunities to visit with their critically ill loved ones.

If you have the time, you might consider offering to serve as "coordinator," finding relatives, friends, and visitors to handle the tasks that require attention. If you elect to undertake this extra dimension of the *bikkur cholim mitzvah*, strive to maintain the family routine as it was before the crisis, particularly if the family includes children. Introduce changes in their routine gradually.

The role of a "coordinator" is particularly useful when a patient faces long-term convalescence or is likely to be permanently homebound. Homebound people are often elderly and living alone or married to someone who has limited physical and economic resources. What may be needed is a surrogate family—a network of aware and concerned individuals, men and women—to share responsibility for the well-being of the invalid.

Often, the best care you can provide for the patient is to assist the caregivers. They need time off. Consider what you might do to relieve them temporarily of some of their responsibilities. Your help is vital (though it may not take the place of necessary and valuable professional services). There is a real need for both volunteer and paid services and for the coordination of them.

In addition to assisting the family with cooking, shopping, transportation, and cleaning, try to support their emotional needs. Give them positive reinforcement at every opportunity.

BIKKUR CHOLIM—AN EGALITARIAN MITZVAH

Tradition stresses the view that everyone should visit the sick. "Even a prominent person must visit a humble one," says the Shulchan Aruch.[35] It follows that the old are obligated to visit the young, the rich the poor, the powerful the less powerful, and vice versa. Also, both men and women should visit, and it is a *mitzvah* to visit non-Jews as well. This may be an opportunity to show respect for religious and cultural diversity. Correct performance of the *mitzvah* is egalitarian and must be woven into the fabric of Jewish living.

CHAPTER III

PARTICULAR CONCERNS FOR VISITORS

A PATIENT'S PHYSICAL CONDITION, AGE, OR MEDICAL TREATMENT MAY POSE special challenges for a visitor, making it difficult to relate comfortably to the person being visited. This chapter considers seven categories of patients identified as creating particular concerns for visitors: children, the terminally ill, persons being treated for cancer, persons with dementia, persons suffering from strokes or spinal cord injuries, persons with acquired immune deficiency syndrome (AIDS), and the homebound elderly.

CHILDREN

Sick children present the visitor with a special challenge. The visitor must observe all the standard rules and also take into account the particular stage of the ill child's development in order to respond appropriately to the needs of the child.

Generally speaking, children are not as pessimistic as their elders. Usually they expect to get well. Support this optimism as firmly as you can without deception. Children are adept at reading signals and will perceive the truth.

Children's needs change as they mature. The preschool child is primarily concerned with separation from parents. The kindergarten and early-elementary school child focuses on bodily changes that the illness or surgical procedure might bring about. The concern that an adolescent usually has about being normal may be exaggerated in the face of illness.

This exacerbated concern over normality is significant because it may complicate the task of establishing an identity. The adolescent also worries about the effect of his or her illness on acceptance by peers and on those relationships which play a major role in adolescence.

Infants require cuddling. Before the age of eight months, they do not strongly differentiate among caregivers. Thereafter they might prefer their mothers but will accept an alternate caregiver, particularly if that person is a frequent visitor. By volunteering to hold a sick infant, you not only give comfort to the child, but respite to the parents.

Toddlers and preschoolers require not only physical comforting but diversion through stories, songs, or games. Plan activities in advance. Often you will have to guess what will appeal to the child. If you do not have access to materials that you think the child might enjoy, investigate the resources in the hospital playroom. If the child longs for a particular activity for which the necessary materials are not at hand, speak with the hospital volunteer guild to see if these materials can be acquired.

Encourage the school-age child to indicate how he or she would like to use your visit. The child might want you to assist with homework and bring supplies, or simply read to him or her. If your visits are frequent and the hospital stay prolonged, consider initiating an ongoing story. If possible, provide the child with materials which can be used when alone or shared with others: a headset and tapes, puzzles, cards, games. Variety is important to a child in the elementary years.

The adolescent patient is perhaps the most difficult to visit. Already hypersensitive to his or her physical condition, the adolescent patient may become upset or angry at any impairment, particularly one that is visible. Let the patient express those feelings, and do not make light of it. Acknowledge the adolescent's frustrations. Focus on the temporary nature of the ailment if possible. If the adolescent (or adult, for that matter) will, in fact, be more or less disfigured or impaired, talk pragmatically about means of making the disability less intrusive over the course of life.

The adolescent may be concerned about social life. It is important to be able to keep in touch with friends, through visits, if appropriate, and through phone calls and letters. Facilitate such contacts.

You can also ensure that the child "keeps up with" peers by assisting with homework and by providing news of the outside world. For example, no adolescent should be without a radio, CD or cassette player, and earphones.

In dealing with the adolescent, ask what you can do in the same way that you would ask an adult, but do so tactfully. It would not be wise to exacerbate the patient's feelings of dependency at the time when he or she is struggling toward independence.

A child might bring up the subject of death. Treat these questions in a straightforward manner. Explain that you are trying to think the issue through because you—like everyone else—have not achieved a complete understanding of the nature and timing of death. Young children often have very concrete concerns: Who will feed my kitten if I die? Urge the child to concentrate on living rather than dying. Tell the younger child that it helps to think positively, and the older child that science has proven that the mind influences the body. Having first secured the permission of the child, you might want to share the child's concerns with the rabbi or social worker.

TERMINALLY ILL PERSONS

When a person is diagnosed with a disease that is likely to result in death, he or she may be said to have a "terminal" illness. But people often live for long periods of time with a disease that eventually ends in death.

Generally, a person is considered terminally ill when the illness has progressed to the point when the focus of care most properly becomes the giving of comfort and the relief of suffering, rather than attempts at eradicating disease. In terms of time, this often comprises the last weeks and months of life. In a hospital setting, the person may be considered terminally ill when death is "imminent," or expected within approximately two weeks. Hospice services, increasingly available within home or hospital settings, are generally offered when a physician expects the person to live approximately six months.

A hospice is dedicated to providing physical, emotional, and spiritual support to those who are facing death. In a hospice the patient and his or her support circle become the focus of compassionate care. Hospice care embraces death as part of life, attempting neither to hasten nor to postpone death, but actively offering support and comfort during this period. Team members include the patient and loved ones, doctors, nurses, social workers, clergy, home health aides, and volunteer visitors. Working together, each strives to value the needs and wishes of the patient and family to empower them to make choices and implement solutions that are right for them. The emphasis is on relief from suffering and enhancement of the quality of life during this significant time of living and dying.

Be aware that the terminally ill individual, like all of us, wants to be regarded as normal. He or she often fears isolation when the news "gets out" that there is no hope for recovery. There may be many months left in a person's life, even when the prognosis is terminal—months of productivity, companionship, and contribution to the self and to the community.

By visiting, you involve this individual with the outside world, and you remind others that it is important to maintain contact. No one, after all, can predict exactly when another will die. Until death is very near, visiting a terminally ill person is an affirmation of life and *kedushah* (holiness).

If possible, you might examine your reactions to life-threatening illness in your friends, your family, and even yourself. There are several reasons why you may fear visiting a person whose prognosis is grave. Frequently a healthy person feels guilty at the prospect of appearing the picture of health to someone who is gravely ill. Many worry that they might say something wrong and cause unnecessary discomfort or anxiety to the patient. Most significantly, visiting a terminally ill person forces the visitor to come to terms with his or her own mortality, often a frightening experience.

Remember that even trained hospice workers frequently have anxiety the first time they encounter a new patient. If you feel queasy or inadequate, you are neither unique nor unworthy of the task.

Resolve to visit, and you will enrich your life and the patient's. If your worst fears are realized and the patient is totally uncommunicative or wretched, your mere presence fulfills the *mitzvah* of *bikkur cholim*.

You often help others—family, friends, hospital staff, roommates—just by coming.

When you visit a terminally ill person you will want to convey a sense of hope. Traditional and modern care-giving practices concur that you help a person establish links to the future by encouraging productive activity during the remaining days of life.

If a patient is experiencing inner turmoil or others around him or her seem frenetic, you can bring a gift of serenity. Your calm demeanor and willingness to sit quietly, listen, or talk soothingly will create a few precious moments of peace and reassurance.

Frequently, medical procedures or increasing physical limitations rob a terminally ill patient of control over many aspects of life. By involving a person in making decisions and by encouraging feelings that these decisions are valid, you help the patient reduce the fear of dependency and actually restore control over certain aspects of life.

When family members are present, you can help them and the patient by listening to them nonjudgmentally and by not intervening in family dynamics. You boost the morale of the family by reassuring them that they are doing a good job of giving care.

Although it is not advisable to initiate conversation about this sensitive, private subject, the terminally ill person may want to talk about death. Or, the patient may prefer not to acknowledge or discuss the fact that he or she is dying, and you should respect these wishes. Follow the patient's lead in sharing feelings and concerns about death and dying.

When specific questions about death arise, it is sufficient to be an active listener. Avoid prognoses; always keep in mind that only God determines the moment of death. If a person expresses concern about the manner of his or her dying, one response may be to assure the patient that there need be no feelings of guilt about leaving loved ones behind.

Offer practical assistance to ease the dying patient's concerns about pressing, unfinished worldly business. For example, you could offer to complete income tax returns or write an important letter.

Consider also the matter of wills. Most of us have prepared a will to dispose of our material possessions. Some of us have executed "living wills" or "advance directives" or "durable powers of attorney" or other such documents giving instructions regarding our medical care. There is a third category of final documents that is to be found in our tradition—Jewish "Ethical Wills." These are documents that articulate those matters which are most important to us as individuals and as Jews, and those values which we wish to leave to our family and friends. There are sources listed in the bibliography which can assist one in the preparation of an ethical will and which give examples of these spiritual legacies. They are very appropriate documents to be written or tape-recorded by visitors as well as families.

You can also ease the patient's mind by offering to relieve the family of obligations that preoccupy them and inhibit their attention to the patient's needs. In addition, your presence can offer the family the opportunity for respite to do errands, attend meetings, or socialize outside of the home.

Finally, when it becomes difficult to bring hope, peace, or meaningful connections to the world of the living, you can simply sit with the ill person, hold hands, and say, "I'm so glad we are together."

CHEMOTHERAPY PATIENTS

The idea of chemotherapy provokes uneasiness in most of us. Perhaps this uneasiness derives from the reverence that people have had for blood throughout the ages; perhaps it is the mistaken notion that chemotherapy is a treatment of last resort. Whatever our fears, they are also the fears of the chemotherapy patient. Frightened over a weakened condition and sensitive to the possibility of being regarded as a pariah, the patient is in particular need of the *mitzvah* of *bikkur cholim.*

Chemotherapy is used to guard against the postoperative recurrence of cancer and to treat advanced or metastatic cancers, which are inoperable because they may be diffused throughout the body. There are approximately fifty chemicals in the modern chemotherapeutic arsenal. These chemicals are administered either orally as pills or liquids, or as liquids infused directly into the bloodstream. The chemicals affect both cancer and normal cells. Whereas normal cells have an inherent capacity to heal themselves, cancer cells do not. The aim of chemotherapy is to destroy cancer cells without damaging the normal cells beyond their capacity for self-healing.

The most quickly dividing cells—the cells of the digestive tract, hair follicles, and bone marrow—are most sensitive to chemotherapy agents. Thus, patients sometimes experience nausea, baldness, and low blood cell counts. Long-term chemotherapy can also damage the kidneys, heart, and lungs.

It is the physician's job to determine when the benefits of chemotherapy outweigh the side effects. The number of therapies used in cancer treatment is increasing, and physicians are becoming increasingly skilled in using them in order to obtain better results with fewer side effects.

A patient receiving chemotherapy in the hospital or clinic or at home may be temporarily affected by the medications. Many individuals undergoing chemotherapy treatment are mobile and functioning but may appear fatigued and drawn. It is important to arrange your visit so that you don't disturb the patient or arrive at an inconvenient time, but do come when a visit would be welcome. Try to provide a reassuring presence, and do not be alarmed at the patient's appearance.

Because some medications cause nausea, do not routinely bring food or aromatic items, but check first to determine what would be appreciated. Since the patient's white blood cell count could be lowered, check before visiting so that if necessary the patient can defer the visit to decrease the chance of catching something from you.

A hospitalized chemotherapy patient may be radically affected by the treatment, so the timing of your visit is very important. Call in advance to make sure that you will be welcome. Prepare yourself for the sight of an individual who may appear severely ill, although the prognosis may, in fact, be very hopeful. Do not reveal pity for the patient; instead give firm support. Regardless of a patient's circumstances, you may want to pray for healing.

Extend support to the family members and caregivers. They (and the patient) may be faced with anything from the shock of a new diagnosis to a recurrence after years of coping with cancer, to the hope of a new cure. By making contact with caregivers you can find out what emotional or physical support could help at this particular time. After a relapse, the family may appear to disengage somewhat from the patient. You, the visitor, can be a kind of buffer in this process, filling in if the family has begun the process of separation.

ALZHEIMER'S PATIENTS

The Talmud is explicit in recognizing the dignity of persons with dementia: "R. Joseph learned: This teaches us that both the tablets and the fragments of the tablets were deposited in the ark. Hence [we learn that] a scholar who has forgotten his learning through no fault of his own must not be treated with disrespect."[36]

Of the various dementias that afflict older adults, Alzheimer's disease is currently the most common. It afflicts millions of Americans. Alzheimer's disease is a physical illness characterized by the loss of certain brain cells, degenerative changes in brain cells, and losses of certain chemical transmitters.

Persons with Alzheimer's disease develop problems in language orientation and performance of simple physical tasks as well as impairments in other brain functions. The disease is characterized by a gradual loss of memory and of mental and physical abilities. This process may take many years. Ultimately, people are incapable of thought, speech, and movement, spending their days in a catatonic state, as helpless as newborns. By the time that an Alzheimer's patient is institutionalized or confined to round-the-clock home care, he or she is unlikely to recognize family members or to be capable of responding to simple statements or questions. Despite these limitations, persons with Alzheimer's disease retain their humanity and individuality until death.

Why take time to visit such a patient? The simple answer is that the Alzheimer's victim, though cut off from society, is still a member of society, deserving of care and attention. Because this individual may be unable to relate a personal history or express present needs, you, the visitor, must do it for him or her. If you do not, the patient could become merely an object in the eyes of a busy nursing home staff. The visitor, by personalizing the patient, helps the often overworked staff to focus on the patient as a worthy individual. The patient will be aware of the warm and caring attitude you express.

When you visit an Alzheimer's patient, proceed in a calm, orderly manner. Be aware that in the earlier stages of the disease the patient may experience mood swings, resulting possibly from frustration or an impending sense of loss. Much agitated behavior is managed with medication. Try to understand the feelings behind the person's language. For example, requests for mother may be understood as a desire for love. You might respond by discussing caring feelings in simple terms. Try not to tell the person that he or she is "mistaken." Be careful not to argue with a confused person. Such correctives may precipitate an angry outburst. Do not take any outbursts personally. Remain calm and request help from the staff if necessary.

Speak slowly to an Alzheimer's patient. Simplify your language. Talk about things in the patient's immediate environment: the meal the staff has set, the pictures on the wall, the sunshine, the plants and flowers growing in the garden. Or talk about the vivid parts of the patient's past: family, close friends, career, or places where he or she once lived. Remind the patient about the events that occurred long ago. Old songs and music are very effective. Try to bring a laugh or at least a flicker of happy memory to the patient's eyes.

Do what you can to make the room a more stimulating place. Hang family photographs or pictures that grandchildren have recently made. See that there is a radio in the room. Hang a mobile. If you bring anything other than food to the patient, see that his or her name is prominently and permanently affixed to the item.

Because the Alzheimer's patient is increasingly reduced to the realm of the physical self, concentrate on physical needs, particularly those needs for which the staff has no time. Walk or wheel the patient up and down the halls or around the grounds. Try playing catch, using a large ball. If the patient was a gardener, plant seeds and guide his or her hands to press the earth down over them. Let the patient hold the hose to water the lawn or garden or lie down in the grass and watch the clouds.

There are few patients for whom touch is more meaningful. Brush the patient's hair. Stroke the arm. Rub the shoulders. Hold hands. Put your arm around him or her as you converse. If appropriate, bring a kitten to hold.

Pay particularly sympathetic attention to the family of the Alzheimer's patient. Some of them will be worn out from caring for their relative. Others will be wracked with guilt over not sharing the burden. Urge the family to express their concerns and to seek mutual support from one of the many support groups or organizations that have sprung up around the country to counsel people in their situation. Indeed, your visit could free caregivers to attend such meetings.

PERSONS WITH STROKES OR SPINAL CORD INJURIES

Stroke victims and persons with spinal cord injuries confront sudden, radical physical and psychological assaults on their customary self-image. Persons with these two conditions have some similar and some very different concerns.

People who suffer trauma such as sudden loss in functional capacity go through multiple stages of adjustment. Initially, patients may experience denial or depression and anxiety. Often, there is the belief that, within a short period of time, the patient will return to full functional capacity. Another stage of the adaptation process is bargaining. The patient feels that if he only works long and hard enough, function will return. The common stages of grief and loss described by the renowned physician Elizabeth Kubler Ross are also common in patients who suffer loss of functional capacity.

When the patient is aware that the body is not working as it should, he or she may become extremely distressed at his helplessness. The patient may try unsuccessfully and with mounting frustration to speak or move his limbs. When it is difficult or impossible to convey feelings or needs, or when the patient feels misunderstood or patronized by others who may view him as less than whole, the patient may lapse into despair.

When you visit a person struggling with complex emotional and physical problems, you need to be very sensitive to his or her inner turmoil. It is important to identify and be genuine about any feelings of distress at sensing suffering or seeing the various unpleasant accouterments of illness, such as a urine bag or intravenous equipment. Your feelings of anxiety are quite natural. Patients don't necessarily want to be cheered up or told that everything is going to be fine. What helps them the most is empathy. If you feel that you don't know what to say, express just that. You may want to say something like "It's okay if we don't have a wonderful conversation. I'm just here to be with you." Do not be surprised if you become upset after you leave the patient, especially if you have suppressed your own feelings of shock or horror during your visit.

There are several steps you can take to prepare yourself emotionally for a visit. It is good to learn as much as you can from the patient's family or nurses about the extent and nature of his or her condition.

Remember that if you visit a person during the acute phases of these illnesses, the extent and permanence of damage has not yet been determined. What you see on your first visit to a stroke or spinal cord injury victim may seem more alarming than is actually warranted over the longer course of recovery.

When you visit, always ask permission before rendering assistance to the patient. By doing this, you recognize the individual's right to control a limited world. If he or she is too sick to respond to your request, then say what you are about to do—plump a pillow, straighten a nightgown, or hold a glass of water—before you actually do it.

If you visit the patient during the rehabilitation phase, it is all right to ask about what he or she is learning or about the progress being made and to commiserate about the process. Physical therapy is extremely challenging and rehabilitation can be slow, but attitude affects progress. A patient must work very hard to achieve each goal. It's always a plus to have these efforts acknowledged.

Although some of the initial emotional reactions of stroke and spinal cord injury patients may be similar, other concerns may be strikingly different, because the two conditions differ markedly in origins, symptoms, and prognoses. If you are aware of some of the unique aspects of strokes and spinal cord injuries before your visit, you may be a more effective visitor.

Strokes. The medical term for stroke is cerebrovascular accident (CVA), which means that a blood vessel in the brain has suddenly ruptured, causing bleeding and damage to surrounding tissue. Because specific parts of the brain control particular functions of the body, damage to these parts results in damage to the bodily functions which they control. Frequently the manifestations of damage are loss of motor control, paralysis or impaired speech, and difficulty in understanding other people's speech. CVA generally affects older persons; its most common precipitant is high blood pressure.

Because of the type of brain injuries caused by CVA, when you visit a stroke patient during the first month of illness you are likely to witness certain behavior that you may find extremely upsetting. Often the stroke patient is groggy and tires easily. He or she may not be able to understand your speech or to translate thoughts into coherent sentences. Emotions, too, may change frequently and inappropriately, causing you to feel as though you have said or done something wrong.

During this early phase, it is advisable to visit for very short periods of time—at most, fifteen minutes. Pay attention to the patient's falling asleep or averting his or her eyes while you are talking. This usually results from trying unsuccessfully to communicate and is not intended as criticism of your efforts.

When you first see the patient, feel free to offer your hand. If the right hand is immobile, you can either touch the impaired limb or, if the left hand is functional, offer to shake it.

Speak slowly. If the patient cannot keep up that end of the conversation, just hold hands. Your presence may be a definite comfort. Remember that he or she is aware of these difficulties. For example, it is all right to provide a word with which the patient may be struggling. You might say, "It's okay if we don't have a conversation; I'm here to be with you."

If the patient struggles with speech, you may manage a simple conversation by encouraging him or her to press your hand with the palm in response to questions requiring yes or no or number-related answers. If you are aware of the patient's interests, you can bring news from that world.

As the patient emerges from the acute phase of illness, certain gifts—Polaroid pictures of family and friends, get-well messages, cassettes, books on tape, or reading material—are particularly appropriate as connectors to his or her former and future life. Check with a nurse before bringing food to a CVA patient. The patient may be on a special diet or have difficulty swallowing and need to be supervised while eating to avoid choking. Do not bring a CVA patient cigarettes. Impaired motor control, judgment, and physical condition make cigarette smoking especially dangerous.

Spinal cord injuries. Damage from a spinal cord injury affects a person's body from the location of the injury down to the toes or arms and, depending on the severity of the injury, may cause some degree of paralysis and loss of motor control.

Unlike strokes, spinal cord injuries most frequently happen to young people. For a significant number of persons, paralysis resulting from spinal cord damage is associated with alcohol- or drug-related automobile accidents. Other causes of spinal cord injuries include swimming pool accidents, certain medical disorders, suicide attempts, and other random mishaps.

Because spinal cord injury is most typically the result of traumatic accident, the individual often ruminates about such matters as "what if." There is often intense self-blame and self-recrimination. The individual may feel that somehow the injury could have been avoided and may take on blame; knowing this may help you to better understand monumental anger at this situation.

Your visit to a person during the acute phase of a spinal cord injury can be very helpful in encouraging a sense of attachment to the world outside the immediate hospital environment. If you are aware beforehand how difficult it is to visit someone in this situation, you can resolve to make your visit upbeat even though you feel sad inside.

The more you are attuned to a patient's vulnerabilities, the more confident you will feel about visiting. There are certain things it is *not* advisable to do:

- Do *not* inquire as to the cause of a spinal cord injury. This is often a very delicate subject, and knowledge of the cause will not make you a more competent visitor.

- Do *not* touch the wheelchair or other mechanical ambulatory equipment without explicit permission. These are extensions of the body over which the patient may be reluctant to share control.

- Do *not* speculate about the likelihood of ever walking again. If the patient brings up the subject, express hope that he or she will walk, and encourage working toward that goal. Stress "one day at a time."

- Do *not* treat the patient as though he or she is mentally impaired or like a child. Any hint on your part, conscious or unconscious, verbal or nonverbal, of lessened competence could result in resentment and rejection of your interest.

Treatment for spinal cord injury is oriented toward helping the patient to be as independent as possible, regardless of the ultimate level of disability. Encourage the patient in his or her rehabilitation regimen and focus on even the smallest successes that have been made in regaining independent functioning.

PERSONS WITH ACQUIRED IMMUNE DEFICIENCY SYNDROME (AIDS)[37]

As the number of people infected with HIV (the virus most widely thought to cause AIDS) continues to increase dramatically, visits to the sick are more likely to include visits to persons with HIV/AIDS. AIDS itself is a syndrome which develops when a person who is infected with HIV starts developing a wide array of opportunistic infections caused by a suppressed immune system. A person living with AIDS is often referred to as a PLWA or PWA (person with AIDS). Although AIDS has become an epidemic that presents a major challenge to the community, you as a visitor should follow the same principles of visiting the sick as you would for anyone else.

Some visitors may be concerned about their own potential health risks when visiting a person with AIDS. In fact, a visitor could pose more harm to the PWA than the PWA to the visitor. For people with compromised immune systems, it is unwise to have visitors who are presenting symptoms of flu, colds, fever, or contagious respiratory problems unless the visitor takes certain precautions. The person with AIDS is susceptible to acquiring the visitor's flu or cold and, in turn, further compromising his or her immune system. If there is any doubt, about communicability the visitor is encouraged to alert the person before visiting or to seek additional information from sources knowledgeable about AIDS.

HIV is difficult to transmit and cannot be spread through casual contact such as hugging or giving someone a gentle kiss. HIV is reported to be transmitted only through contact with certain body fluids from an infected person, for example, blood or blood products, semen and vaginal fluid, fecal matter, or excretions from an infected area. As a casual visitor, it is unlikely that you would need to wear special garments, because you will not be taking special risks. If you plan to become more involved with the daily care of a PWA, it is imperative that you learn the proper precautionary measures and procedures for caring for someone with AIDS.

Individuals infected with HIV may live many years without experiencing any debilitating health problems. Some of the diseases and infections associated with AIDS can be successfully treated. The AIDS patient therefore realistically can hope to be restored to good health for a limited period once the immediate infection is cured or is in remission. However, once a person's immune system starts declining significantly, he or she may begin to succumb to pneumonias, dementia, rare cancers, and a variety of opportunistic infections. Depending on the course of the disease, some of these cancers and infections may drastically change the appearance of the person. As the disease progresses, it is not uncommon for the person to feel uncomfortable about physical appearance or to show signs of depression, fear, and sometimes anger.

The prognosis for each person with AIDS is unique. Although the image of a person with AIDS as being emaciated and critically ill is sometimes accurate, the person may seem in good health at the time of your visit. Let the PWA's state of health and mental outlook shape the way you approach him or her. A PWA in stable condition and hopeful of recovery will convey a message different from that of the critically ill patient who is resigned to approaching death. It is not your responsibility to help the ill person accept the reality of his or her fate.

Although the populations first noted to be infected with HIV in the United States were homosexual men and IV drug users, recent statistics indicate that HIV infection in the U.S. is most rapidly increasing within the heterosexual population. Largely due to the specific populations originally infected in this country, there has been considerable stigma surrounding those living with AIDS. Some PWA's must not only deal with the diagnosis and prognosis of AIDS, but also with the judgment of others who may hold them in contempt.

The source of infection is irrelevant to your visit. Trust your normal instinct, listen to what the person with AIDS is saying, and avoid being judgmental. Think of the purpose of your visit. You are there to provide comfort and assistance to someone who is ill. For example, the person with AIDS may need religious advice in planning for death and may ask you to find a rabbi. He or she may need support in breaking the news of this diagnosis to family or friends, or in resolving other family issues.

Supporting and caring for someone who is ill with AIDS is not an endorsement of a way of life that may be different from your own. Honesty and compassion, constructive dialogue, and perhaps a willingness to understand will build rapport which will provide crucial emotional support.

HOMEBOUND AND CHRONICALLY ILL INDIVIDUALS

Any person suffering from a debilitating condition from which he or she is not likely to recover may exhibit certain disquieting attitudes or behavior. This may occur particularly during the early phases of chronic illness, while the individual struggles to adjust to the reality of new physical limitations. He or she may suffer a loss of self-esteem that diminishes the ability to cope and to relate to others.

The crisis of illness and day-to-day uncertainty about future recovery may induce a psychological imbalance such as depression or anxiety. A person may feel permanently different and, frequently, inferior. As a visitor, you help to provide the support necessary for the chronically ill person of any age to regain or sustain a positive self-concept. On regaining self-esteem, a person is better able to manage and influence the surrounding world. In short, an improved self-concept is critical to long-term adjustment to chronic disability.

You will help yourself cope with difficult visits by trying to understand the problems with which the patient is contending. By grasping the individual's dilemma, you may even help him or her to lessen this malaise, manage anxiety, or reduce fear.

The promise of regular visits through which a homebound person can establish or enrich a relationship with another is immensely valuable. If you are planning to pay regular visits to a homebound person who is also elderly, it is important to review your own attitudes about aging. In our society, most people view aging negatively. Although some people accept gracefully the inevitability of growing older, others deny or fear the aging process. Honest appraisal of your own perceptions will help you to determine whether you can undertake such visits with an open mind.

For the most part, the homebound elderly are philosophical about their limitations and are reluctant to impose their very real physical problems on you, particularly if you are a casual visitor. Older persons, for physiological and psychological reasons, may have a reduced capacity to adapt to change. At the same time, because they have had more experience with coping and more exposure to various types of adversity, they may have developed certain coping skills not available to younger persons.

You can help the homebound person by encouraging activities that increase independence or provide opportunities for interaction. Even if severely restricted in movement, he or she might tend to plants, play cards, write poetry, or do volunteer telephoning for a charitable organization. The homebound person, whose contact with the outside world may be shrinking, enjoys receiving telephone calls and mail.

There is a unique pleasure in spending time with an alert elderly person of limited physical mobility. If you undertake such a visit, try to set aside adequate time to spend listening and responding. If, however, you have a limited amount of time available, visit anyhow, and explain that you can only stay for a short time. The older, essentially homebound person has a different concept of time from people whose main preoccupations are work, child rearing, or going to school. Such a person takes time to talk, to pour a pot of tea, to share photographs and hobbies. When you enter this world, be prepared, if possible, to respect his or her internal clock.

An elderly person may have considerable life experience to share and few people left with whom to share it. This may be because friends have died or the family lives elsewhere and cannot visit regularly. As a visitor, you help relieve feelings of isolation and powerlessness. You can learn a great deal about an individual's life and about the history, literature, attitudes, and culture of earlier times simply by engaging the person in conversation.[38]

CHAPTER IV
THE CAREGIVER AND THE PHYSICIAN

THE CAREGIVER

Once, when the sage Hillel had finished a lesson with his pupils, he accompanied them partway home.

"Master," they asked, "where are you going?"

"To perform a religious duty," he answered.

"What duty is that?"

"To bathe in the bathhouse."

"Is that a religious duty?" they asked.

"If somebody is appointed to scrape and clean the statues of the king that stand in the theaters and circuses, is paid for the work, and even associates with nobility," he answered, " how much the more so should I, created in the image and likeness of God, take care of my body!" (Leviticus Rabbah 34,3).

Since by keeping the body in health and vigor one walks in the way of God—it being difficult during sickness to have any understanding or knowledge of the Creator—it is one's duty to avoid whatever is injurious to the body and cultivate habits conducive to health and vigor (Maimonides Code, "Laws Concerning Moral Dispositions and Ethical Conduct" 4,1).

THE PHYSICIAN

Judaism affirms that we inhabit a body that belongs to God. As a consequence, we are responsible for its care through prevention and cure, and when this is not possible, through palliation and understanding support. The physician's efforts to heal and comfort are not perceived as a denial of God's prerogatives, but rather as a duty.[39] The physician is God's partner in maintaining health and in relieving the pain of the sufferer.

The following general principles apply:

- The better informed a patient is, the easier it usually becomes to cope with reality. Uncertainty tends to foster anxiety and feelings of loss of control.

- The patient has a legal and ethical right to know the truth. Patients who want to know will generally ask direct questions. Such questions should be answered directly and honestly. When possible, answers should include hope for improvement even if the improvement relates only to symptoms.

- Respect denial. Patients who do not wish to know will ordinarily not ask questions. We should be prudent in providing unrequested information. Some patients may deny the reality of their situation in order to protect their emotional integrity. This must be respected.

- According to Jewish law, it is permissible at times to withhold facts about a patient's condition, if that will contribute to the welfare of the patient. In truth, most dying patients do not expect miracles. What they ask for most of all is confirmation of our care and concern.

- The needs of the patient are primary. Decisions as to sharing information about the patient's condition with family should be determined within the principle of confidentiality.[40]

PRAYER FOR THOSE WHO HELP

May the One who blessed our ancestors be present to those who provide help for the ill and troubled among us. May they be filled with fortitude and courage, endowed with understanding, sympathy, and compassion as they give strength to those at their side. May they fight against despair, and continue to find within themselves the will to reach out to those in need. And in their love of others, may they know the blessing of community, and the blessing of renewed faith.

CHAPTER V

CONCLUSION

As you visit the sick—listening to their concerns, talking with them, laughing and praying together, holding one another—keep in mind that you are experiencing rare moments, closer to the core of human experience than most moments you encounter in the hurly-burly of daily life. Learn from your experience in the sickroom. Reflect on what is important in life. Consider your own priorities. Think about the meaning of friendship in general, and the particular friendship that you are confirming or forging in the performance of the *mitzvah*.

Feel enriched and empowered by the *mitzvah* of *bikkur cholim*. For indeed, the benefit flows not only to the person who is ill, but to you, the visitor. It is as if you were the one who asked the patient, "Give me your hand," and rose up stronger and straighter because of the touch.

APPENDIX 1—PRAYERS

1. *Mi Sheberach*— Traditional Prayer for Healing

May the One who blessed our ancestors, Sarah and Abraham, Rebecca and Isaac, Leah, Rachel, and Jacob, bless _____ son/daughter of _____ and _____ along with all the ill among us. Grant insight to those who bring healing; courage and faith to those who are sick; love and strength to us and all who love them. God, let Your spirit rest upon all who are ill and comfort them. May they and we soon know a time of complete healing, a healing of the body and a healing of the spirit, and let us say: Amen.

—FROM THE SIDDUR

For a male:

מִי שֶׁבֵּרַךְ אֲבוֹתֵינוּ, אַבְרָהָם יִצְחָק וְיַעֲקֹב, שָׂרָה רִבְקָה רָחֵל וְלֵאָה,
הוּא יְבָרֵךְ וִירַפֵּא אֶת הַחוֹלֶה _____ בֶּן _____ . הַקָּדוֹשׁ בָּרוּךְ הוּא
יִמָּלֵא רַחֲמִים עָלָיו, לְהַחֲזִיקוֹ וּלְרַפְּאוֹתוֹ, וְיִשְׁלַח לוֹ מְהֵרָה רְפוּאָה
שְׁלֵמָה לְכָל אֲבָרָיו וְגִידָיו בְּתוֹךְ שְׁאָר חוֹלֵי יִשְׂרָאֵל, רְפוּאַת הַנֶּפֶשׁ
וּרְפוּאַת הַגּוּף (שַׁבָּת הִיא מִלִּזְעוֹק / יוֹם טוֹב הוּא מִלִּזְעוֹק /
וּרְפוּאָה קְרוֹבָה לָבוֹא) הַשְׁתָּא בַּעֲגָלָא וּבִזְמַן קָרִיב, וְנֹאמַר אָמֵן.

For a female:

מִי שֶׁבֵּרַךְ אֲבוֹתֵינוּ, אַבְרָהָם יִצְחָק וְיַעֲקֹב, שָׂרָה רִבְקָה רָחֵל וְלֵאָה,
הוּא יְבָרֵךְ וִירַפֵּא אֶת הַחוֹלָה _____ בַּת _____ . הַקָּדוֹשׁ בָּרוּךְ הוּא
יִמָּלֵא רַחֲמִים עָלֶיהָ, לְהַחֲזִיקָהּ וּלְרַפְּאוֹתָהּ, וְיִשְׁלַח לָהּ מְהֵרָה
רְפוּאָה שְׁלֵמָה לְכָל אֲבָרֶיהָ וְגִידֶיהָ בְּתוֹךְ שְׁאָר חוֹלֵי יִשְׂרָאֵל,
רְפוּאַת הַנֶּפֶשׁ וּרְפוּאַת הַגּוּף (שַׁבָּת הִיא מִלִּזְעוֹק / יוֹם טוֹב הוּא
מִלִּזְעוֹק / וּרְפוּאָה קְרוֹבָה לָבוֹא) הַשְׁתָּא בַּעֲגָלָא וּבִזְמַן קָרִיב,
וְנֹאמַר אָמֵן.

2. Mi Sheberach—Alternate Version

Source of mercy, spread Your shelter of peace over all the ill among us and watch with special care over _____. Help us, as we seek ways of healing; share Your kindness with us, that the bonds of love and caring be increased; and grant courage and hope to the sick and the well together. Reveal Your compassion and Your blessing upon all who are ill and comfort them. Speedily and soon, let us see together a day of complete healing, a healing of body and a healing of spirit, and let us say: Amen.   —FROM "SERVICE OF HEALING," RUACH AMI, SAN FRANCISCO

3. Mi Sheberach—
Music by Debbie Friedman
Lyrics by Debbie Friedman and Drorah Setel

מִי שֶׁבֵּרַךְ אֲבוֹתֵינוּ, מְקוֹר הַבְּרָכָה לְאִמוֹתֵינוּ

Mi sheberach avoteinu, m'kor habracha l'imoteinu:
May the Source of strength who blessed the ones before us
Help us find the courage to make our lives a blessing
And let us say: Amen.

מִי שֶׁבֵּרַךְ אֲבוֹתֵינוּ, מְקוֹר הַבְּרָכָה לְאִמוֹתֵינוּ

Mi sheberach imoteinu, m'kor habracha l'avoteinu:
Bless those in need of healing with *refuah shelaymah*
The renewal of body, the renewal of spirit
And let us say: Amen.

4. A Prayer for Visitors to Recite

Source of Healing of the Universe,
   in whose hands are the issues
   of life and health,
Grant complete healing
   to _____,
   along with all those who suffer.
Impart your wisdom
   to those who care for the sick.

To the family
  of _____,
  give strength enough for each day.
To us,
  the members of his/her community,
  grant understanding
  and a caring heart,
So that we may be there when he/she needs us.
Return him/her to us, we pray,
  sound in body and whole in spirit,
  in perfect health,
To do your will.

— RABBI AVIS D. MILLER, ADAS ISRAEL CONGREGATION, WASHINGTON, D.C.

5. From the Siddur

Blessed are You, Adonai, Creator of the universe, who has made our bodies in wisdom, creating openings, glands and organs, marvelous in structure, intricate in design. Should but one of them, by being blocked or opened, fail to function, it would be difficult to stand before You. Praised are You, source of our health and strength, we give You thanks and praise.

בָּרוּךְ אַתָּה יהוה אֱלֹהֵינוּ מֶלֶךְ הָעוֹלָם, אֲשֶׁר יָצַר אֶת הָאָדָם בְּחָכְמָה וּבָרָא בוֹ נְקָבִים נְקָבִים חֲלוּלִים חֲלוּלִים. גָּלוּי וְיָדוּעַ לִפְנֵי כִסֵּא כְבוֹדֶךָ שֶׁאִם יִפָּתֵחַ אֶחָד מֵהֶם אוֹ יִסָּתֵם אֶחָד מֵהֶם אִי אֶפְשָׁר לְהִתְקַיֵּם וְלַעֲמֹד לְפָנֶיךָ. בָּרוּךְ אַתָּה יהוה רוֹפֵא כָל בָּשָׂר וּמַפְלִיא לַעֲשׂוֹת.

6. A Litany for Healing

We pray that we might know before whom we stand: the Power whose gift is life, who quickens those who have forgotten how to live.

We pray for winds to disperse the choking air of sadness, for cleansing rains to make parched hopes flower and to give all of us the strength to rise up towards the sun.

We pray for love to encompass us for no other reason save that we are human—that we may all blossom into persons who have gained power over our own lives.

We pray to stand upright, we fallen; to be healed, we sufferers; we pray to break the bonds that keep us from the world of beauty; we pray for opened eyes, we who are blind to our authentic selves.

We pray that we may walk in the garden of a purposeful life, our own powers in touch with the power of the world.

Praise to the God whose gift is life, whose cleansing rains let parched men and women flower toward the sun.

—FROM "SERVICE OF HEALING," RUACH AMI, SAN FRANCISCO

7. The Priestly Blessing (Numbers 6:24-26)

May God bless you and guard you

May God show you favor and be gracious to you

May God show you kindness and grant you peace.

יְבָרֶכְךָ יהוה וְיִשְׁמְרֶךָ.

יָאֵר יהוה פָּנָיו אֵלֶיךָ וִיחֻנֶּךָ.

יִשָּׂא יהוה פָּנָיו אֵלֶיךָ וְיָשֵׂם לְךָ שָׁלוֹם.

8. From the *Amida*

Heal us, Adonai, and we shall be healed. Help us and save us, for You are our glory. Grant perfect healing for all our afflictions. May it be Your will, Adonai our God and God of our ancestors, to send complete heal-ing of body and soul, to _____ along with others who are stricken. For You are the faithful and merciful God of healing. Praised are You, Adonai, Healer of the people of Israel.

רְפָאֵנוּ יהוה וְנֵרָפֵא, הוֹשִׁיעֵנוּ וְנִוָּשֵׁעָה כִּי תְהִלָּתֵנוּ אַתָּה. וְהַעֲלֵה רְפוּאָה שְׁלֵמָה לְכָל מַכּוֹתֵינוּ.

On behalf of someone ill, you may add:

יְהִי רָצוֹן מִלְּפָנֶיךָ יהוה אֱלֹהֵינוּ וֵאלֹהֵי אֲבוֹתֵינוּ, שֶׁתִּשְׁלַח מְהֵרָה רְפוּאָה שְׁלֵמָה מִן הַשָּׁמַיִם, רְפוּאַת הַנֶּפֶשׁ וּרְפוּאַת הַגּוּף, לְ_____ בֶּן/בַּת_____ בְּתוֹךְ שְׁאָר חוֹלֵי יִשְׂרָאֵל.

כִּי אֵל מֶלֶךְ רוֹפֵא נֶאֱמָן וְרַחֲמָן אַתָּה. בָּרוּךְ אַתָּה יהוה רוֹפֵא חוֹלֵי עַמּוֹ יִשְׂרָאֵל.

9. From the Siddur

בְּשֵׁם יְיָ אֱלֹהֵי יִשְׂרָאֵל   In the name of Adonai:

מִימִינִי מִיכָאֵל.   May the angel Michael be at your right

וּמִשְׂמֹאלִי גַּבְרִיאֵל.   and the angel Gabriel be at your left;

וּמִלְּפָנַי אוּרִיאֵל.   and in front of you the angel Uriel

וּמֵאֲחוֹרַי רְפָאֵל.   and behind you the angel Rafael

וְעַל רֹאשִׁי   and above your head

שְׁכִינַת אֵל.   the *Shechinah* (Divine Presence).

10. Psalms

Another way to pray for the sick is to recite specific Psalms that engender hope, such as Psalms 6, 9, 13, 16, 17, 20, 22, 23, 25, 30, 31, 32, 33, 37, 38, 39, 41, 42, 49, 51, 55, 56, 59, 69, 77, 86, 88, 90, 91, 102, 103, 104, 105, 107, 116, 118, 121, 130, 137, 142, 143, 148, or 150. These may be said in any language and either by the visitor or together with the sick person. A wonderful resource is *Healing of Soul, Healing of Body*, edited by Simkha Y. Weintraub (see Bibliography) in which spiritual leaders unfold the strength and solace in selected Psalms.

A different custom is to choose verses from Psalm 119 that spell out the individual's name, the mother's name, and the words: *kera satan* (may the evil decree be abolished). Since Psalm 119 is an acrostic containing verses beginning with each letter of the alphabet, this is a unique way to tailor a prayer to an individual. This is typically followed by a *Mi Sheberach* (above).

11. Names

In many communities it is customary to use the name of the mother of the sick person instead of the father. The reason often given for this custom is that the Hebrew word for compassion is *rachamim* and the Hebrew word for womb is *rechem*. We ask that God give protection and be compassionate just as the mother's womb gave love and compassion.

In the event of serious illness, there was a custom to give an additional name (usually of someone who had lived a long life) to the sick person. This folk custom was intended to confuse the Angel of Death who would be unable to know the new person's name and so could not claim the soul. This is viewed as a re-birth. This name change usually follows the recitation of Psalm 119, after which the following lines are said:

And his/her name in Israel shall be called: (new name).

(For a male): As it is written: "And you shall no longer be called Abram, but your name shall be Abraham, for I made you the father of a multitude of nations." (Genesis 17:5)

(For a female): As it is written: "As for your wife Sarai, you shall not call her Sarai, but her name shall be Sarah." (Genesis 17:15)

May it be Your will, Adonai our God and God of our ancestors, that the change of this name make naught all harsh and evil decrees; tear away from him/her the evil decisions. If death was decreed upon (old name), but on (new name) it was not decreed. If harm was decreed upon (old name), but on (new name) there is no such decree. She/he is like a different person, a newborn individual. Like an infant born to good life, length of years, and fullness of days, as it is written : "I have heard your prayer, I have seen your tears. I hereby add fifteen years to your life" (Isaiah 38:5).[41]

12. *Vidui*—Confession

Our tradition has a prayer of confession which should be recited by the rabbi or elder family member together with the person who is so severely ill as to be near death. This does not mean that all hope for recovery is lost, rather that the recitation of this confession should ease the mind and reduce the anxiety while at the same time asking for God's forgiveness. Various forms such as this one exist:

My God and God of my ancestors, accept my prayer; do not ignore my supplication. Forgive me for all the sins which I have committed in my lifetime. I am abashed and ashamed of the wicked deeds and sins which I committed. Please accept my pain and suffering as atonement and forgive my wrong-doing, for against You alone have I sinned.

May it be Your will, Adonai my God and God of my ancestors, that I sin no more. With Your great mercy cleanse me of my sins, but not through suffering and disease. Send a perfect healing to me and to all who are stricken.

Unto you, Adonai, my God and God of my ancestors, I acknowledge that my life and recovery depend upon You. May it be Your will to heal me. Yet if You have decreed that I shall die of this affliction, may my death atone for all sins and transgressions which I have committed before You. Shelter me in the shadow of Your wings; grant me a share in the world to come.

Father of orphans and Guardian of widows, protect my beloved family, with whose soul my own soul is bound.

Into your hand I commit my soul. You have redeemed me, Adonai, God of truth.

Hear O Israel, Adonai is our God, Adonai is one.

Adonai, He is God. Adonai, He is God.

אֱלֹהַי וֵאלֹהֵי אֲבוֹתַי, תָּבֹא לְפָנֶיךָ תְּפִילָּתִי וְאַל תִּתְעַלַּם מִתְּחִנָּתִי. אָנָּא, כַּפֶּר לִי עַל כָּל-חַטֹּאתַי שֶׁחָטָאתִי לְפָנֶיךָ מֵעוֹדִי עַד הַיּוֹם הַזֶּה. בּוֹשְׁתִּי וְגַם נִכְלַמְתִּי כִּי הִסְכַּלְתִּי לַעֲשׂוֹת מַעֲשִׂים רָעִים וַחֲטָאִים. וְעַתָּה, קַח נָא עָנְיִי וּמְרוּדִי לְכַפְּרָתִי, וּמְחַל לִמְשׁוּבָתִי, כִּי לְךָ לְבַד חָטָאתִי.

יְהִי רָצוֹן מִלְּפָנֶיךָ, יְיָ אֱלֹהַי וֵאלֹהֵי אֲבוֹתַי, שֶׁלֹּא אֶחֱטָא עוֹד, וּמַה שֶּׁחָטָאתִי לְפָנֶיךָ, מָרֵק בְּרַחֲמֶיךָ הָרַבִּים, אֲבָל לֹא עַל יְדֵי יִסּוּרִים וַחֳלָיִם רָעִים. וּשְׁלַח לִי רְפוּאָה שְׁלֵמָה עִם כָּל-חוֹלֵי עַמְּךָ יִשְׂרָאֵל.

מוֹדֶה (מוֹדָה) אֲנִי לְפָנֶיךָ, יְיָ אֱלֹהַי וֵאלֹהֵי אֲבוֹתַי, שֶׁרְפוּאָתִי וּמִיתָתִי בְּיָדֶךָ. יְהִי רָצוֹן מִלְּפָנֶיךָ, שֶׁתִּרְפָּאֵנִי רְפוּאָה שְׁלֵמָה. וְאִם גָּזַרְתָּ שֶׁאָמוּת מֵחֳלִי זֶה, תְּהִי מִיתָתִי כַּפָּרָה עַל כָּל-חֲטָאִים וַעֲוֹנוֹת וּפְשָׁעִים שֶׁחָטָאתִי וְשֶׁעָוִיתִי וְשֶׁפָּשַׁעְתִּי לְפָנֶיךָ. וְתַסְתִּירֵנוּ בְּצֵל כְּנָפֶיךָ, וְאֶזְכֶּה לְחַיֵּי הָעוֹלָם הַבָּא.

אֲבִי יְתוֹמִים וְדַיַּן אַלְמָנוֹת, הָגֵן בְּעַד קְרוֹבַי הַיְקָרִים אֲשֶׁר נַפְשִׁי קְשׁוּרָה בְּנַפְשָׁם.

בְּיָדְךָ אַפְקִיד רוּחִי, פָּדִיתָה אוֹתִי יְיָ, אֵל אֱמֶת.

שְׁמַע יִשְׂרָאֵל, יְיָ אֱלֹהֵינוּ, יְיָ אֶחָד.

יְיָ הוּא הָאֱלֹהִים. יְיָ הוּא הָאֱלֹהִים.

סֵדֶר וִדּוּי REPRINTED BY PERMISSION OF THE RABBINICAL ASSEMBLY FROM *A RABBI'S MANUAL* EDITED BY RABBI JULES HARLOW (PP. 96-98). COPYRIGHT BY THE RABBINICAL ASSEMBLY, 1965.

To be said by the rabbi if the patient is unable to do so

Adonai our God and God of our ancestors, we acknowledge that our life is in Your hands. May it be Your will that You send perfect healing to _____. Yet if it is Your final decree that he/she be taken by death, let it be in love. May his (her) death atone for the sins and transgressions which he (she) committed before You. Grant him/her of the abundant good which is held in store for the righteous, and give him/her life replete with joy in Your Presence, at Your right hand forever.

Father of orphans and Guardian of widows, protect his (her) beloved family, with whose soul his/her own soul is bound. Into your hand he/she commits his/her soul. You have redeemed him/her, Adonai, God of truth.

Hear O Israel, Adonai is our God, Adonai is one.

Praised be the glory of God's sovereignty for ever and ever.

Adonai is King; Adonai was King; Adonai shall be King for ever and ever.

Adonai, He is God. Adonai, He is God.

מוֹדִים אֲנַחְנוּ לָךְ, יְיָ אֱלֹהֵינוּ וֵאלֹהֵי אֲבוֹתֵינוּ, שֶׁחַיֵּינוּ מְסוּרִים בְּיָדֶךָ. יְהִי רָצוֹן מִלְּפָנֶיךָ, שֶׁתִּרְפָּא אֶת הַחוֹלֶה הַמְּסֻכָּן הַזֶּה (וְהַחוֹלָה הַמְּסֻכָּנָה הַזֹּאת) רְפוּאָה שְׁלֵמָה. וְאִם הַמָּוֶת כָּלָה וְנֶחֱרַץ מֵעִמְּךָ יִקָּחֵנוּ (יִקָּחֶהָ) מִיָּדְךָ בְּאַהֲבָה. וּתְהִי מִיתָתוֹ (מִיתָתָהּ) כַּפָּרָה עַל כָּל חֲטָאִים וַעֲוֹנוֹת וּפְשָׁעִים, שֶׁחָטָא וְשֶׁעָוָה וְשֶׁפָּשַׁע (שֶׁחָטְאָה וְשֶׁעָוְתָה וְשֶׁפָּשְׁעָה) לְפָנֶיךָ. וְתַשְׁפִּיע לוֹ (לָהּ) מֵרַב טוּב הַצָּפוּן לַצַּדִּיקִים וְתוֹדִיעֵהוּ (וְתוֹדִיעֶהָ) אֹרַח חַיִּים, שֹׂבַע שְׂמָחוֹת אֶת-פָּנֶיךָ, נְעִימוֹת בִּימִינְךָ נֶצַח. אֲבִי יְתוֹמִים וְדַיַּן אַלְמָנוֹת הָגֵן בְּעַד קְרוֹבָיו (קְרוֹבֶיהָ) הַיְקָרִים אֲשֶׁר נַפְשׁוֹ (נַפְשָׁהּ) קְשׁוּרָה בְּנַפְשָׁם. בְּיָדְךָ יַפְקִיד רוּחוֹ (תַפְקִיד רוּחָהּ), פָּדִיתָ אוֹתוֹ (אוֹתָהּ) יְיָ, אֵל אֱמֶת, אָמֵן וְאָמֵן.

שְׁמַע יִשְׂרָאֵל, יְיָ אֱלֹהֵינוּ, יְיָ אֶחָד.

בָּרוּךְ שֵׁם כְּבוֹד מַלְכוּתוֹ לְעוֹלָם וָעֶד.

יְיָ מֶלֶךְ, יְיָ מָלָךְ, יְיָ יִמְלֹךְ לְעוֹלָם וָעֶד.

יְיָ הוּא הָאֱלֹהִים. יְיָ הוּא הָאֱלֹהִים.

סדר וידוי REPRINTED BY PERMISSION OF THE RABBINICAL ASSEMBLY FROM *A RABBI'S MANUAL* EDITED BY RABBI JULES HARLOW (PP. 96-98). COPYRIGHT BY THE RABBINICAL ASSEMBLY, 1965.

13. *Birkat Hagomel*—Giving Thanks

Birkat Hagomel is recited in the synagogue upon receiving an *aliyah* after recovering from a serious illness, surviving a harrowing trauma, or successfully undergoing surgery or difficult treatments:

Praised are You, Adonai our God, ruler of the universe, graciously showing kindness to those in Your debt, even as You have bestowed favor on me.

בָּרוּךְ אַתָּה יהוה אֱלֹהֵינוּ מֶלֶךְ הָעוֹלָם, הַגּוֹמֵל לְחַיָבִים טוֹבוֹת שֶׁגְּמָלַנִי כָּל טוֹב.

Baruch atta Adonai, eloheinu melech haolam, hagomel lachayavim tovot, shegemalani kol tov.

The congregations responds:

May God who has been gracious to you continue to favor you with all that is good.

מִי שֶׁגְּמָלְךָ (שֶׁגְּמָלֵךְ) כָּל טוֹב, הוּא יִגְמָלְךָ (יִגְמָלֵךְ) כָּל טוֹב סֶלָה.

Mi shegemalcha (shegemalech) kol tov, hu yigmalcha (yigmalech) kol tov sela.

14. Alternate Prayer upon Recovery

I give thanks to You, Adonai my God, faithful healer of the sick. You gave me strength to bear pain and affliction. You have given me new spirit and hope.

I am grateful to You, Adonai my God, for all the messengers of healing; for those whose medical skills and patient care aided me; for all those who helped speed my recovery by kind words and deeds of friendship and affection.

Continue to be with me during the days of my convalescence. Help me be cheerful and to bear with patience whatever discomforts I may have.

I pray that I may carry out the worthy resolutions which I made during my illness.

May I always value the blessing of health; and in gratitude for Your healing, may I do the utmost in helping to preserve the health and well-being of others.

—FROM PRAYERS FOR HEALING, PRAYER BOOK PRESS OF MEDIA JUDAICA

APPENDIX 2—
A CHECKLIST OF DO'S AND DON'TS FOR VISITORS

The Initial Visit

DO

- ❏ Visit sick friends or strangers after the crisis period of the illness has passed.
- ❏ Call or write a note before coming if you do not know the patient well.
- ❏ Call again if the patient does not wish to see you initially. This simply may be a bad day.
- ❏ Familiarize yourself with the patient's condition, if possible, so that you do not appear surprised if he or she is disfigured or disabled.
- ❏ Enter the room with something to talk about that will interest the patient.
- ❏ Leave a note if, when you visit, the patient is asleep or out of the room.
- ❏ Bring a little gift.
- ❏ Relax yourself into a visiting mode by concentrating on your visit, so that you can truly "be present."

DON'T

- ❏ Be afraid of doing something wrong.
- ❏ Wear perfume or shaving lotion, as illness often heightens a person's sense of smell.
- ❏ Make elaborate plans for your initial visit.
- ❏ Insist on visiting if the patient repeatedly asks you not to visit.
- ❏ Wear a depressed face.

Appropriate Time to Visit

DO

- ❏ Visit during hospital hours or, at home, during the early afternoon to early evening, unless the patient requests otherwise.
- ❏ Visit on the Sabbath and holy days.

Length and Frequency of Visits

DO

- ❏ Visit a patient both at the hospital and after returning home.
- ❏ Suggest that you come another time, if the patient has visitors.
- ❏ Step out of the room if the doctor wants to examine the patient.
- ❏ Visit frequently, if possible.

DON'T

- ❏ Stay long, unless the patient requests it.

Listening

DO

- ❏ Listen actively by questioning and acknowledging what the patient is telling you.
- ❏ Let the patient's anger come out without taking it personally.
- ❏ Remember that you are there as a friend and do not have to make things better.
- ❏ Keep matters confidential if that is the patient's desire.

DON'T

- ❏ Question the doctor's judgment on the diagnosis or treatment, even when the patient does.

- [ ] Take sides in a patient's expressions of anger about family or friends.
- [ ] Change the subject. As tough as it may be for you, try to hear him or her out.

Talking

DO

- [ ] Watch and listen for clues from the patient regarding the desire for conversation.
- [ ] Talk about the patient's world beyond the sickroom.
- [ ] Try to create a sense of hope and meaning.
- [ ] Let the patient know that he or she matters and that you and the community care.

DON'T

- [ ] Feel that it is necessary to talk with the patient all the time you are visiting.
- [ ] Be afraid to laugh with the patient.
- [ ] Initiate discussion of a patient's medical condition or the possibility of death. Instead, follow his or her lead.
- [ ] Talk about a patient who appears unable to hear, in that patient's presence.
- [ ] Tire the patient.
- [ ] Offer platitudes or speak as if you know God's plans.
- [ ] Talk about your own illnesses or troubles.

Prayer

DO

- [ ] Pray in a sick person's presence, but only if he or she requests it.

- ❏ Pray so that the patient can hear and understand you.
- ❏ Pray for the patient outside of his or her presence.
- ❏ Feel free to formulate your own personal prayers, or use a commonly accepted prayer in the prayer book.
- ❏ Conclude the visit with the words: May you have a *refuah shelaymah.*

Touching the Sick Person

DO

- ❏ Ask the patient whether you may touch him or her, if you are in doubt.
- ❏ Offer to hold hands, brush hair, or touch in other non-threatening ways.

DON'T

- ❏ Touch a patient's wheelchair, walker, or other medical paraphernalia without asking permission.

Sitting with the Patient

DO

- ❏ Position yourself so that the patient can see you without strain.
- ❏ Sit at the same level.

DON'T

- ❏ Sit on the bed without asking the patient's permission.
- ❏ Communicate a desire to get away.

Tending to Tangible Needs

DO

- ❏ Discover how you can be of tangible assistance to the patient.
- ❏ Offer to help only with things that you are actually able to perform.
- ❏ Offer help to patients both in the hospital and at home.
- ❏ Be sensitive to the ways in which you can help the patient's family.

DON'T

- ❏ Insist on helping if the patient or family indicate that they don't need your help.
- ❏ Decide for the patient or his family what sort of help they most need.
- ❏ Offer to do more than you are able to do.
- ❏ Try to "fix" it.

END THOUGHTS

RABBI BRADLEY S. ARTSON,
CONGREGATION EILAT, MISSION VIEJO, CALIFORNIA

Many times during the year I go to the hospital to visit sick people. I go in order to pray and in order to give a bit of strength and support if I can. But nine times out of ten I come away heartened and encouraged and inspired and informed by what the patients who are there teach me. Let me tell you what I have learned. So far, I have never yet heard a patient in the intensive care unit or in the recovery room say to me: rabbi, I made a mistake, I should have earned more money. Or, rabbi, I made a mistake, I shouldn't have spent so much time with my kids. Nobody has ever said that to me yet. Instead, what they say to me is what Isaac said: if I get better, I am going to be smarter. If I get better, I am going to run around less and I am going to meditate more; or, if I get better, I am going to fight less and I am going to give more; or, rabbi, if I get better, I am going to make more time to be with my wife. This is what people tell me when they come out after they have been under the knife. ("Under the Knife." In *The World of the High Holy Days*, edited by Jack Riemer. Miami: Bernie Books, 1992.)

RABBI RACHEL COWAN,
NATHAN CUMMINGS FOUNDATION, NEW YORK

I had always thought that visiting sick people was important and I tried to do it as often as I could. But, like most Jews I didn't see it as a *mitzvah* in the sense of "commandment." Instead I preferred to translate *mitzvah* as "good deed"—something a nice person does when he or she feels up to it. The year I spent with Paul during his illness—six months of that time in hospitals, sleeping in his room many nights, keeping him company and boosting his spirits—made me understand the importance of the *mitzvah*. If people do not have visitors, they find it much more difficult to mobilize their spirit and energy and to promote their healing, to engage in the drive to overcome their illness, or to live as fully as possible in the face of it. In that time, I also came to understand what our tradition has long taught—that Jews depend upon community, and that community is built through very specific, nitty-gritty, practical actions. Community cannot exist meaningfully when Jews hand over to rabbis the task of caring for each other's rejoicing and praying and healing and mourning. (*CLAL—Perspectives*, 5, no. 3. September 1990.)

RABBI BILL CUTTER, HEBREW UNION COLLEGE, LOS ANGELES

Illness can be understood as a hollowness, not the presence of an invader but the pressure of emptiness: an absence of coherence, of relationship and of confidence in the underpinnings of our lives. It is a kind of sudden *tzimtzum* with its accompanying vacuum. Our minds are conditioned to expect fullness: love, occupation, satisfaction at the table. So illness is a visitation which surprises and makes us ask, "Why me? Why now? Where have I gone?" For me, then, the sick patient must work on filling the space—the sudden void, and the speechlessness when the news comes down from the medical staff that an emptiness of health has occurred. (*CCAR Journal*, Summer 1992.)

RABBI NANCY FLAM, RUACH AMI, SAN FRANCISCO

Perhaps disease has nothing to do with merit or demerit, and is simply a necessary though sometimes agonizingly painful feature of this physical creation...*Midat hadin* (the divine attribute of *din* [judgment]), then, carries within it the necessity of limits and finitude. Disease and death are expressions of *midat hadin*. Physical bodies are limited; they are created with a finite capacity for life and health. They are vulnerable to disease, injury, and decay. We are created and, without exception, pass away. This is part of God's holy design...Whereas illness expresses *midat hadin*, healing expresses *midat harachamim* (the divine attribute of mercy)...Our human acts of mercy, compassion, and empathy make it possible for us to endure, to suffer the sometimes excruciatingly painful limits and losses of creation...the Jewish impulse is to add to the principle of *rachamim* so that it might outweigh, indeed ideally, messianically, overcome the power of *din*...Acts ° *rachamim* may not only make the limits more bearable, but may 'ally affect the limits themselves. (*Sh'ma* 24/475. May 27, 1994.)

RABBI ABRAHAM JOSHUA HESCHEL, z'l

Sickness, while primarily a problem of theology, is a crisis of the total person, not only a physical disorder. There is a spiritual dimension to sickness. At a moment in which one's very living is called into question…the ultimate question of what it means to be alive [is] of…importance. ("The Patient as Person." *Conservative Judaism*, Fall 1964.)

RABBI HAROLD KUSHNER,
NATICK, MASSACHUSETTS

We don't have to beg or bribe God to give us strength or hope or patience. We need only to turn to the One, admit that we can't do this on our own, and understand that bravely bearing up under long-term illness is one of the most human, and one of the most godly things we can ever do. One of the things that constantly reassures me that God is real, and not just an idea that religious leaders made up, is the fact that people who pray for strength, hope. and courage do so often find resources of strength, hope, and courage that they did not have before they prayed. (Personal communication, 1996.)

RABBI HAROLD SCHULWEIS,
VALLEY BETH SHALOM, ENCINO, CALIFORNIA

[I have experienced] confusion, denial, anger, despair, and dark fear. [He reminds us that when we visit the sick we need not come armed with great wisdom or advice. What the sick need is a presence and a loving ear.] Some say that there are no atheists in intensive care units and none in the waiting rooms of hospitals. I don't believe that. To be scared into faith is to inherit a sick faith. The fear will not last, nor will the faith. But faith may come out of a crisis because it bends the tin of your iron will. When the debris and the clutter of the armored self clear away you may begin your rediscovery. Old-new questions reappear. What and who and when is the most important in your life? These questions call for self-revelation and for confessional. This moment, this hour, this day is the most important. Do you know whether you will have another like this one? Do not neglect the present tense. (Personal communication, 1996.)

RABBI ALEXANDER SHAPIRO, z"l

Writing in *Conservative Judaism*, Rabbi Shapiro dwells on the fears that filled him, and the utter sense of loneliness that engulfed him, especially during the initial stages following his heart attack. He tells us that he is busily engaged in converting the curse of his illness into a blessing. "I find myself far more in touch with my own body and the world around me than ever before in my life. There is an exhilaration with which I greet the morning sun that was never there before...There is something in the sight of a beautiful tree that touches something in my soul in a way that I never felt before...I take time for myself. I take long walks daily, drinking in the beauties of God's world; I exercise religiously, and I have learned to do something rabbis are supposed to do though I never knew how—to spend time in sheer contemplation of the universe...I no longer have to work sixteen hours a day to be worthy of love. I find myself more sensitive to pain and human frailty and somehow more responsive." During his illness, his wife kept a verse from Psalms near the telephone: *vaani bechasdecha batachti*, I trust in Your lovingkindness. ("A Rabbi and His Family." *Conservative Judaism*, Fall 1981.)

RABBI MILTON STEINBERG, z"l

In a sermon, "To Hold with Open Arms," Steinberg describes an emotional paradox: he urges himself and us "to hold the world tight—to embrace life with all our hearts and all our souls and all our might." But after urging us to hold the world tight, he goes on to remind us that ultimately we have to give it up. One moment we are urged to hold open and in the next breath we are told to be prepared to let go. We resolve this paradox by our faith in God. If we believe in God, everything becomes more precious because it is a divine gift and a reflection of divinity. And if we believe in God, it is also easier to let go. (Rabbi Milton Steinberg, *A Believing Jew*. New York: Harcourt Brace, 1951.)

RABBI JEFFREY A. WOHLBERG,
ADAS ISRAEL CONGREGATION, WASHINGTON, D.C.

A scholar of the Talmudic period, Simon the Just is known for having taught that one of the three pillars on which the world rests is the pillar of *gemilut chasadim*, acts of loving-kindness. In his view, together with study of Torah and worship, these acts sustain the world. There are of course, many ways of expressing kindness and love. Most noble and meaningful among them are those acts which exemplify sensitivity, which lift the spirit, which inspire confidence and instill hope. *Bikkur cholim*, the act of visiting those who are not well, is among the most beautiful. Those who perform this *mitzvah* may not actually bring about healing, but they provide something equally necessary if health is to be regained: they calm the spirit and engender a feeling of warmth. It is ironic that during this age of enormous strides in the technology of healing, there are so many who complain about the impersonality of the process. *Bikkur cholim* is personal. It is compassionate. It helps overcome the loneliness and fear which so often accompanies illness. (First edition of *Give Me Your Hand,* 1988.)

RABBI DAVID WOLPE,
JEWISH THEOLOGICAL SEMINARY, NEW YORK

The same God who decided that it is not good to be alone, made it so that we can never completely escape that fate…loneliness is the seal of creation. Bounded by bodies, we pass the days meditating, musing, dreaming; but we reveal only a small fraction of our inner life to those around us. Most of what passes through our minds, and our hearts, is never shared. We are not born with the recognition of our loneliness. Children do not know the difference between their thoughts and the thoughts of others. They do not understand internal and external. Everything and everyone seems to dwell inside the mind. But one day each of us says a magic word: "I." The first meaning of "I" is "not you." We are separate, unique—alone…So where can we turn in our aloneness? Judaism teaches that loneliness is ultimate only in the absence of God. God can see inside us, can understand us at levels that elude our friends, our family—even our own selves. God overflows boundaries, and assures us that we are not alone. (*Sh'ma.* 24/457, September 1993.)

NOTES

1. Rabbi Tzvi Blanchard, *Joining Heaven and Earth: Maimonides and the Laws of Bikkur Cholim* (New York: National Center for Jewish Healing, 1994).

2. Deuteronomy 13:5.

3. Genesis 1:26.

4. Genesis 18:1.

5. Talmud Sotah 14a. (All Talmud references are to the Babylonian Talmud.) To perpetually commemorate that event, we continue to observe the Shabbat of Parshat Vayera, where this biblical story of Abraham occurs, as the day set aside to honor those in the *Bikkur Cholim* Society.

6. Daily morning prayer, based on Mishnah Peah I.

7. Shulchan Aruch 335.

8. A wonderful description of a medieval Jewish community which engaged in the *mitzvah* of visiting the sick is portrayed in Israel Abrams' *Jewish Life in the Middle Ages*, (Philadelphia: Jewish Publication Society, 1958). 329–331

9. Talmud Nedarim 40a.

10. Talmud Berachot 5b.

11. Talmud Nedarim 39b and elsewhere.

12. Shir Hashirim Rabba 11:16.

13. Shulchan Aruch 335:2 (Isserles gloss).

14. Based on Deuteronomy 4:15 ('For your own sake, therefore be most careful').

15. Shulchan Aruch 335:8, based on Talmud Nedarim 41a.

16. Shulchan Aruch 335:8.

17. Talmud Berachot 5b.

18. Talmud Nedarim 40a. One Talmudic rabbi, Raba, actually discouraged visitors on the first day because he believed that visits would call attention to a person's illness and cause deterioration. But even Raba acknowledged the importance of informing the community of illness by the second day.

19. Avot 11:16.

20. Shulchan Aruch 335:4, based on Talmud Nedarim 40a.

21. Talmud Nedarim 39b.

22. Shulchan Aruch 335:8.

23. Shir HaShirim Rabba 11.

24. Ibid.

 Shulchan Aruch 335:4 (Isserles gloss).

  ulchan Aruch 335:4, based on Talmud Sotah 33a.

[27] Shulchan Aruch 335:6.

[28] Ibid.

[29] Prayerbook *Vidui.*

[30] "At Bedside." (Palm Springs, Calif.: National Institute for Jewish Hospice).

[31] Nahum Waldman, "Bikkur Holim." In *Celebration and Renewal*, ed. Rela Geffen (Philadelphia, Pa.: Jewish Publication Society, 1993).

[32] Zohar on Pinchas. The Zohar, the thirteenth-century tract that is the key to Jewish mysticism, distinguishes between ordinary and righteous invalids. It teaches that the *Shechinah* surrounds the righteous invalid, and consequently a visitor can only sit at his feet.

[33] Shulchan Aruch 335:7.

[34] Shulchan Aruch 335:2, based on Babylonian Talmud Nedarim 39b.

[35] See Judith Fitzgerald Miller, *Coping with Chronic Illness* (Philadelphia, Pa.: F. A. Davis Co., 1983).

[36] Talmud Menachot 99a.

[37] This section in the first edition was written by the late Steven Weisberg, a volunteer at the Whitman Walker Clinic, Washington, D.C.

[38] See Judith Fitzgerald Miller, *Coping with Chronic Illness.*

[39] Exodus 21:19.

[40] This note to physicians was taken from *Caring for the Jewish Terminally Ill—A Primer,* published by the National Institute for Jewish Hospice, Los Angeles.

[41] Meyer Strassfeld, "Visiting the Sick." In Strassfeld and Strassfeld, *The Third Jewish Catalogue*, comps. and eds. Sharon Strassfeld and Michael Strassfeld (Philadelphia, Pa.: Jewish Publication Society, 1980).

BIBLIOGRAPHY

At Bedside. Palm Springs, Calif.: National Institute for Jewish Hospice, n.d.

Making Contact. Washington, D.C.: Candlelighters Childhood Cancer Foundation, 1987.

Caring for the Jewish Terminally Ill—A Primer. Los Angeles, Calif.: The National Institute for Jewish Hospice, n.d.

Blanchard, Rabbi Tzvi. *Joining Heaven and Earth: Maimonides and the Laws of Bikkur Cholim.* New York: National Center for Jewish Healing, 1994.

Geffen, Rela, ed. *Celebration and Renewal.* Philadelphia, Pa.: Jewish Publication Society, 1993.

Jaffe, Rabbi Hirschel; Rudin, James; and Rudin, Marcia. *Why Me? Why Anyone?* New York: St. Martin's Press, 1987.

Kushner, Harold S. "The Spiritual Dimensions of Improving the Quality of Life: How the Rabbi Helps." In *Proceedings of the First National Conference on Hospice for the Jewish Community.* New York: Synagogue Council of America, 1984.

———*When Bad Things Happen to Good People.* New York: Schocken Books, 1981.

Miller, Judith Fitzgerald. *Coping With Chronic Illness.* Philadelphia, Pa.: F. A. Davis Co., 1983.

Rabin, Roni. *Six Parts Love.* New York: Charles Scribner's Sons, 1986.

Reimer, Jack. *Jewish Insights on Death and Mourning.* New York: Schocken Books, 1996.

Reimer, Jack. *Jewish Reflections on Death.* New York: Schocken Books, 1974.

Schur, Rabbi Tsvi F. *Illness and Crisis / Coping the Jewish Way.* New York: National Council of Synagogue Youth, Union of Orthodox Jewish Congregations of America, 1987.

Schulweis, Harold. "The Art of Visiting the Sick." *Baltimore Jewish Times,* n.d.

Strassfeld, Meyer. "Visiting the Sick." In *The Third Jewish Catalogue,* compiled and edited by Sharon Strassfeld and Michael Strassfeld. Philadelphia, Pa.: Jewish Publication Society, 1980.

Weintraub, Simkha Y., ed. *Healing of Soul, Healing of Body.* Woodstock, Vt.: 'ewish Lights, 1994.